T0161796

SPARTAN STRONG

What it Takes to Overcome Every Obstacle

Featured as #TEAMKØ on NBC's
Spartan Ultimate Team Challenge

**Bethany Marshall & Jessica Burton
Zac Allen & Andres Encinales**

NEW YORK

LONDON • NASHVILLE • MELBOURNE • VANCOUVER

SPARTAN STRONG
What it Takes to Overcome Every Obstacle
Featured as #TEAMKO on NBC's Spartan Ultimate Team Challenge

© 2018 **Bethany Marshall, Jessica Burton, Zac Allen, Andres Encinales**

Published in New York, New York, by Morgan James Publishing. Morgan James is a trademark of Morgan James, LLC. www.MorganJamesPublishing.com

The Morgan James Speakers Group can bring authors to your live event. For more information or to book an event visit The Morgan James Speakers Group at www.TheMorganJamesSpeakersGroup.com.

ISBN 978-1-68350-129-9 paperback
ISBN 978-1-68350-130-5 eBook
ISBN 978-1-68350-131-2 hardcover
Library of Congress Control Number: 2016909838

Cover Design by:
Rachel Lopez
www.r2cdesign.com

Interior Design by:
Bonnie Bushman
The Whole Caboodle Graphic Design

In an effort to support local communities, raise awareness and funds, Morgan James Publishing donates a percentage of all book sales for the life of each book to Habitat for Humanity Peninsula and Greater Williamsburg.

Get involved today! Visit
www.MorganJamesBuilds.com

SPARTAN STRONG

CONTENTS

THIS OBSTACLE COURSE CALLED LIFE

The four of us—Bethany Marshall, Zac Allen, Jessica Burton, and Andres Encinales—were named Team KO when we appeared on NBC's show *Spartan: Ultimate Team Challenge* as a competing team in 2016.

We first met because of our martial arts training. We share a love of Muay Thai, Brazilian jiu-jitsu, and Mixed Martial Arts (MMA). We also began running obstacle course races (OCR) together, and when we learned of the new Spartan OCR TV show, we knew we had to join together and apply for the show as a team.

At first glance Team KO's common thread is our love for martial arts and OCR, but on a deeper level it is that we have all overcome major life obstacles, such as cancer or poverty, and emerged stronger on the other side.

While the struggles help define us individually, overcoming those life obstacles and the methods we used to do so was what truly united the four of us as a team.

Together we are on a mission to expand Team KO to a movement that motivates people to face difficult life obstacles head-on and rise above their own unique life challenges and obstacles.

We decided to write this book to let our authentic stories be available to others and to share strategies from our journeys.

The following chapters will offer 18 qualities that Team KO uses both in OCR and everyday life. Each chapter includes a space for you to join Team KO as you reflect on and embrace these qualities in your own life.

Out of all the qualities and advice we hope you take away from this book, here's the biggest thing you need to know: obstacles will present themselves in life. We cannot control that. The only things we can control are our own actions and *re*actions to the circumstances we face. The qualities covered in these chapters can be used as tools for keeping control of your actions and reactions. If hearing our stories can help even one person, the vulnerability is worth it. This is who we are.

But the decision to live with these qualities in mind is a choice only you can make.

Meet

#TEAMKO

Bethany Marshall

Bethany Marshall is a professional MMA fighter (4-1) and a Spartan racer. She was a contestant on season one of *Spartan: Ultimate Team Challenge* on NBC in 2016, as well as on season eighteen of *The Ultimate Fighter*, the first season of the show to include women. Bethany is passionate about writing, health, publishing, and helping others in their athletic journeys.

Zac Allen

Zac is an MMA fighter, Spartan racer, cancer survivor, and entrepreneur. As a former wrestler for more than fifteen years, he transitioned naturally into the sport of MMA. He applies the same intensity he brings to fighting to his OCR training. He enjoys challenging himself both physically and mentally, whether it be in preparation for his next fight, race, or business venture.

Jessica Burton

Jessica Burton, also known as "Jess No Limits," is a proud mom and experienced obstacle course racer. She also practices Muay Thai and Brazilian jiu-jitsu. Her goal is to inspire and help anyone in need of a lifestyle change. She has overcome a very dark place in life, as well as other big obstacles in life, and wants to show the world that they can do the same. Jess grew up in Gloucester, Virginia, and currently lives in the Hampton Roads area.

That being said, there's still this B*tch (also referred to as an "inner voice" throughout the book)—a voice inside everyone's head that they battle 24/7. Disclaimer: although the team has tried to think of a different name for that voice, nothing quite captures its nature like B*tch. It's the voice that tells people they're still not good enough, they're failing, they'll never amount to anything, targeting whatever it is each person most fears. With everything that happens in life, it's hard to recognize the B*tch, and most people don't know how to deal with it. Whether you believe that or not, that voice is inside our head. Always. Without the right tools, it has the potential to drown you.

Andres Encinales

Andres Encinales is a martial artist in Brazilian jiu-jitsu and Muay Thai as well as an OCR athlete, certified fitness trainer, and specialist in fitness nutrition through the International Sports Sciences Association (ISSA). He is from New Jersey and moved to Virginia due to his active-duty military status. Andres is a highly motivated athlete who always challenges himself, and hopes to help others reach their highest potential.

FACING FEAR

There is only one thing that makes a dream
impossible to achieve: the fear of failure.
—**Paulo Coelho**, *The Alchemist*

What Does Facing Fear Mean to Team KO?

Fear is an emotion like any other. It tells you that you're not good enough. That you're not capable. That you will fail. Fear is a lie. Facing your fear is a necessary act of defiance that allows you to meet your goals—it's taking back control.

Jess

When I was thirteen, the harsh reality of death interrupted my world.

Three of my friends and I went to a Saturday night Rock N Bowl to celebrate a birthday: me, my best friend Jennifer, and two other friends, one of whom was old enough to drive. It was late when we finished bowling. My parents didn't know we were out. We were acting out, sneaking out, and I was supposed to be sleeping at Jennifer's house.

We decided to go for a drive—not drinking or anything, just joyriding. Jennifer and I fought over the passenger seat, so we settled it by having me sit on her lap. We were young and dumb—just out having a good time.

Then our friend lost control of the car.

He had taken a curve too fast, and we flew into the trees, hitting them head-on. We flipped a few times and ended up upside down. When rescue teams came, we had to be cut out of the car.

I don't know how I made it when Jennifer didn't.

The pain and constant, aching hurt were so real. I couldn't fix what happened, so I crafted a hard shell around the gnawing ball of pain inside me. Since I couldn't destroy the pain, I locked it away, kept it in an impenetrable jail. I lived my life the way I wanted to, regardless of the consequences.

That mode of thinking led to a string of bad decisions that spiraled all the way through my twenties. All that time I refused to deal with any type of pain, instead adding it to my little jail cell inside, hoping it never broke free.

Living through that accident so early in life made me realize how very real death was, and I understood what true heartache meant. I made a turn for the worse trying to escape that realization and the memory of that night—the images seared into my memory. My mom sent me to a counselor and I refused to say a word; I thought there was nothing to talk about. What did they want me to say? She's dead? She's gone? Nothing I could say to a counselor would change what happened. I learned how to suppress what I was feeling, bottling those emotions, and I continued building a wall to keep any pain away from my consciousness.

Now, looking back, I understand what I was doing in an entirely different way. I never wanted to *live* through that pain. I refused to feel it, face it. And that initial refusal created a habit of suppressing fear and pain for years. You know, people saw me as the strong person—the one who never let anything get to her. But I wasn't.

I am now; I wasn't then.

All through my twenties, I continued that destructive pattern. I suppressed what I was feeling and chose to let any base emotions that slipped through the cracks dictate my daily actions. It sent me spiraling into a really bad place (what I refer to as my dark place). I think fear is such a big concept in my life because I chose to drown my fear for so many years, and that's a hard habit to break. The pattern continued when I had my son at a young age and then married a man I didn't love—a man who joined the military, leaving me to face parenthood alone while he was in training. I was scared to death.

So I started having a glass of wine before bed to ease into the night and forget how scared I was. As time went on, it turned into more than just a glass.

Maybe I was just scared of being alone, but ultimately I was running from the fear itself: fear of being alone, fear of failure, fear of being nobody, fear of being a bad mom—all these different fears circling in my mind like vultures ready to prey on my weaknesses. And when I drank, I didn't care what I did. I could drown all those fears in alcohol, suppressing them instead of facing what I was afraid of, washing them behind a wall where they festered for years. It worked. At least until I woke up the next morning.

Then, in 2013, I went out onto the Wintergreen Spartan course after another one of my regular drinking binges. I did the whole race, but when I crossed the finish line suddenly it hit me: I was so disappointed in myself—disappointed in the person I was. As that raw truth sank in, I knew I had to turn things around or I was going to end up killing myself.

After that moment of awareness, I may have drunk once or twice, but within a week I entered myself into a writers' group, and I haven't touched a drink since then. The writers' group was by no means rehab, but it was a tool for facing my emotions and the fears I had suppressed for so very long. It was a way for me to step toward living fully again.

Only now can I see clearly what drove my behavior for so long. It was fear. Fear was my determining factor.

People ask me all the time what made me see the light and work toward getting out of my dark place, and the answer is death. I would have killed myself by continuing down that road, and it was only by God's grace that it didn't happen before I made the choice to change. When you're drunk like I often was, you don't care. You'll take an entire bottle of sleeping pills. Only by God's grace did I make it through alive . . . *only by God's grace.*

Nowadays, the way I overcome fear is by facing it head-on and powering through all the way to the finish line. The choice to face fear is what led me to try both Spartan racing and Muay Thai.

A lot of people don't understand what there is to be afraid of when you go out to run an obstacle course race. For me, the whole time I'm out on that course I struggle with fear. I fear quitting. I fear not finishing. I fear failure. And fear of failure is the biggest fear I face—actually one I have to embrace. Fear of failure is allowed to dictate the lives of so many people. One of the biggest life changes that came when I turned things around was not allowing fear or other base emotions to dictate what I do every day. The only way for me to grow is if I instead face that fear and push past whatever it is that I'm afraid of.

Now it might sound like I've got fear all under control, but it is something I still must face every single day and every single race. When I line up at the starting line with pro athletes, I constantly wonder what I'm doing there. I question my right to be there every step of the way to the finish line.

What are you doing, Jess?
You can't keep up.
I'm going to fail…
I'm going to fail…

My breaking point came during a 2015 DC Spartan Sprint when I was particularly afraid. Not only was I lining up with pro athletes on the starting line, but I was also competing against people I had trained with. I went out there having trained really hard for this race, and I failed *multiple* obstacles, watching one elite woman after another pass me on the course.

When you fail multiple obstacles, it just makes you want to quit.

When you fail one, okay. When you fail two, okay, even three. I think I failed six. Which meant 180 burpees. It's an enormous mental challenge not to think and believe *I'm not in it anymore; why don't I just quit?*

That race was a devastating blow for me. But the thing about OCR is that when you compete, you don't ever know what's going to happen. Every course will be different. You can go out there and give the best you have, and sometimes another racer will beat you. That DC race was my breaking point because I felt like I had failed. It took all my effort to release everything I was doing and recognize that I didn't actually fail because I didn't quit. Quitting and giving up are the only true failures that exist.

Going into my next race, I knew that the same thing that happened at the DC Sprint could happen again, but I decided not to care. I had already beaten the fear once when I thought I was going to quit and kept going. I finished the race. So I went into that next race (and it was one of the hardest races that's on the map for Spartan—Wintergreen), and it turned out to be one of my best races.

After that, I felt like I was free.

Now I know the only way I can fail is if I choose not to try. So I try. I push past the fear and the doubts, and I battle my way to the finish line. And you know what? I go back and look at my placements and I'm placing top 20. I mean, the first year I competed I earned my coin to the world championship. If I had let the fear drive me, I *never* would have been able to do that. I would have given up before I even had a chance.

But let me emphasize again that my war with fear is not over. I still face it every single day. Going into *Ultimate Team Challenge*, there was a huge fear factor. I thought there was no way I could actually do it. My anxiety came from not knowing what I was walking into. I thought I might have a heart attack at that show start line. I mean, I literally felt like that. Emotions were just all over the place. You have to slow it down. You have to focus and tell yourself that you *can* do this. You won't die. And if you do die, at least you'll die trying.

That is the biggest point for me. Unless I'm dead, I will continue to try. I will not quit. Ever. I was at the starting line for *Ultimate Team Challenge* thinking, *Am I going to die?* My heart was beating out of my chest, and I just kept telling myself: *you can do this, you can do this, you can do this, you can do this.*

When it finally started, I remember running past the start line realizing that it was really happening. And then it was race time. I blocked out my surroundings and just kept moving forward no matter what. I had to think about that finish line every single step I took.

When I think about that race now I remember my mind going through an argument with myself:

You can quit.
No, you can't.
Yes, you can.
You have a team.
But what if you have a heart attack?

It's a matter of drowning the B*tch. It's A or Z for me, and anything between those two options are things I've already done in my twenties, which clearly were not the answer.

The truth is that no matter how hard facing my fears can be, I would rather be dead than go back to where I was. That life of suppressing fear is death to me. People want to know how I got to where I am today, and death is still the answer. It's this or die. Sink or swim. Face the fear or be consumed by it.

Andres

With obstacle course racing, whether you win or not, completing the course is an accomplishment in itself. The race acts as more of a self-challenge in that way. You are free to go at your own pace, and if you have to stop, you can stop. That doesn't make the race easy though. It's still a challenging sport because you put your body through incredibly stressful situations and environments. During races, you're hungry. You're thirsty. Muscles and bones ache. You have the option to quit and call for help at any point.

Or you could finish the race.

That's the choice you have to make out on the course. Whenever your body starts to break down, your mind soon follows. Your body is telling you to take a break and screaming out for help and relief.

But that doesn't mean your body isn't capable of pushing forward.

In those moments, you realize just how strong your body really is, and how strong your mind can be too, if you can get your negative thoughts under control.

You get a lot of negative thoughts when your body starts to break down.

I can't do it... It's too hard... I should probably quit...

You have to find a way to fight those thoughts and keep going. Over time, you realize that it doesn't matter how much pain you're in; your mind is the one in charge. When you feel pain in every step you take, it doesn't mean you can no longer run. You can still push yourself to do it, to keep running, to keep moving through the pain. It all depends on how much discomfort you can withstand mentally without breaking.

Fighting in the ring also tests your mental limits, even though the intensity might be a different kind. Not only is it demanding in that moment, but there's also a lot of work leading up to the day of the actual fight. Most people don't see that preparation and mental stamina. All they see is how the fight goes. They don't see you training every single day, from the good days to the bad. Maybe you try a new technique and it's not working, or you're not focused and your training opponents keep beating you.

You still get up the next day and do it all over again.

And you can be focused all you want, but at some point you have to acknowledge that external sources can and will affect your training. If you have problems with work, family, social life, etc., it becomes hard to focus and find the motivation for training—weeks of training to reach a top fitness level so that you can perform at your best in the twelve minutes you have. The length of any competition, whether fighting or racing, can't even compare to the time invested in preparation. With fighting in particular, not only is the time pressure a factor, but you are fighting in front of a crowd, in front of thousands of people. You're literally one of two people in the spotlight. People see every little move that you make. They will either admire or criticize what you're doing.

It's hard being under that kind of scrutiny.

If you go out there and give the fight all you've got, and the crowd does nothing but criticize you, it can be humiliating. It can destroy you. Even if you've never experienced that humiliation yourself, fear of humiliation gets inside your head. You think about your opponent, but you also think about yourself. You've trained for this fight and you know what you're capable of, but seeing that crowd can bring on this incredible state of nervousness.

You step into the cage and across from you, maybe you see a crazy guy with a mohawk, or a guy with a nasty look on his face, and you realize just how badly this fight could turn out.

I had to learn to take those moments and turn them around by reminding myself that I'm no punk. My opponents may look real tough externally, but I have to remember that all of them bleed and sweat just like I do. They train in a gym just like I do. They train in the same arts, at the same level. I've trained with people who compete at my level, and I've trained with those who rank higher than me. I've dealt with that pressure. Sure, acknowledging your opponent's ability is important to stay in the reality of the fight, but it's really about finding a balance between a healthy sort of fear and self-confidence.

If you go out to compete and start getting nervous, stop and remember just what you're capable of. It's all about being confident: trust what you know and what your coaches and instructors have taught you, and lean on the support from your family and your team.

If your opponent is successful, it's because he (or she) was confident in his technique and his art. Whether or not my opponent actually knows more, I go into the cage confident and don't back down for anything.

When you step into a fight, everyone's eyes are on you and you don't know what's going to happen. At first the fights are about being the best and beating your opponents. But after a while, even with all eyes on you, it becomes more about fighting yourself—trying to gain control of yourself—because it can get frustrating during a fight.

I've had fights where I've gotten frustrated and made mistakes, and I've had fights that I lost to guys I know I could have beaten, fights I lost because mentally I lost focus and made mistakes. That's the battle that no one sees.

The audience only sees the external fight or the external race. They don't see what goes on inside, and the losses from your past that pop into your head every time you step up to go again. The question is whether you can stay focused when you're fighting someone and you're exhausted and you're out of breath, and you're being attacked by an opponent who won't give you time to breathe between punches, or when you're racing and you feel like you can't possibly take another step.

Can you keep going, keep fighting?

Despite the challenge, eventually you learn to control yourself in those stressful environments. And that control applies to everything: obstacle course racing, martial arts, work, family. They all influence each other, and learning how to behave in stressful situations and control your decisions applies to all parts of life. The specific actions for each situation may be different, but break down the basic principles and it's all the same.

When you're in a fight, you train yourself to focus and stay calm and move past the fear instead of letting it cripple you. If something bad happens to a family member, you have to control yourself in order to think clearly.

It's a matter of fighting fear, and it's a matter of taking back the reins.

Facing Fear Every Day

It's time to take back control and push through fear rather than let it keep you from accomplishing your goals. Write down one goal that fear is keeping you from accomplishing, and pinpoint what you are afraid of. Then ask yourself: is the fear truly greater than the goal?

_____

_____

_____

_____

_____

_____

_____

_____

_____

_____

_____

_____

_____

_____

_____

_____

_____

_____

_____

_____

ENGAGING MENTAL TOUGHNESS

Rule your mind or it will rule you.
—**Buddha**

What Does Engaging Mental Toughness Mean to Team KO?

Mental toughness is controlling your inner dialog and still prevailing, regardless of your emotions and circumstances. It's easy to be mentally tough when things are going well. It's when times are hard that you must engage your mind and remind yourself that you control your thoughts and actions.

Andres

My family lived in Colombia from when I was nine to fifteen years old. Throughout that time, my dad was a subject no one touched—I spent ten years without any contact with him. Nothing. Nobody asked me about him. Regardless of what anyone else in the family might have known, I never talked about my dad. But that didn't mean I never thought about him.

Often I would sit alone and wonder, *What happened? Why did he leave?* All these thoughts bombarded me: *Did he not love me? Did I do something wrong?*

It was hard to deal with what felt like rejection from a parent, especially at such a young age. As a child, that situation can be hard to interpret, and all the more so when no one talks about it. I'm the type of person who keeps to myself and suppresses my feelings—another reason I never asked or talked about my dad. Sharing my feelings was not my instinct. But even though I never talked about him, there were nights when I was on my own, thinking about him and crying.

Fast forward to fourteen-year-old me.

One day I got out of school and walked home with a friend like I usually did. It was about 7:30 at night because of the way the schools were set up in Colombia. My friend lived a little farther than I, but we were walking together in the same direction, just walking and talking. My older brother and sister were already living in the States, my sister having just left Colombia a couple of months earlier.

An hour later, I finally got home and headed upstairs. My mom was in her room talking on the phone and told me that I had a phone call. Trying to be funny, she teased, "You have an important international phone call."

I assumed it was my brother. "Oh, that's Geo."

"Nope, not him."

"Oh, then it's Vanessa," I responded, which would have been kind of weird because my sister hadn't kept in touch since she moved to the States.

"Nope, it's not her. It's somebody else."

At that point, my guess finally leaped to my dad. It's crazy that my dad was the third option that came to mind, but to be fair, even that was rare since he was someone I hadn't heard from or even spoken about in years. I said nothing, but took the phone and said hello into the receiver.

The guy on the other end asked, "Do you know who you're talking to?"

"Is this my dad?"

After he said yes, I became speechless. I started crying immediately and handed the phone back to my mom because I was choking up. I couldn't say another word. The call was unexpected and out of nowhere, and I didn't know what to say. A few days later, I calmed down and actually had a conversation with him, and I discovered that I had more siblings—a whole family I didn't know about.

After reconnecting with my dad, I went back to the United States in March 2004—New Jersey—where my brother, sister, and dad were all waiting for me at the airport.

Right then I decided not to hold a grudge against my dad. I hadn't seen him in over ten years. Those were ten years lost, ten years I couldn't get back, ten years I didn't have a father, and that relationship was something that I wanted. I decided to leave it all in the past and start anew. I lived with my brother Geo because it would have been too awkward to try to live with my dad, but I would go visit him on weekends, and we slowly rebuilt our previously nonexistent relationship.

The decision to leave everything in the past took a lot of mental toughness, as did rebuilding our relationship. I could have decided to let it end with that phone call, but if I hadn't had the mental toughness to move back to the United States, I never would have gotten to know my dad.

Zac

Some guys are great at fighting—as long as they're winning.

Let me first acknowledge: losing is hard to deal with. Even before actually stepping into the cage, training and cutting weight and focusing intensely for an extended amount of time is hard.

You get to a point in training where you start talking to yourself to keep going and stay on track. Sometimes it's not even internal anymore; sometimes you literally talk out loud to yourself just to keep going. You have to actively converse with that other side of you—that side that wants you to quit. Maybe talking to yourself sounds a little embarrassing, but I don't think in that focused state any of us would notice if someone were making fun of us. Worrying about looking weird or being embarrassed just doesn't matter anymore. It's like no one else is even around. And the thing that sets fighters apart from other athletes is that we go out and test ourselves physically and mentally in ways that no one else does.

You do so much to get your body and mind ready for a fight—weeks of training for a nine- to twelve-minute competition—and you go and just leave it all out there. As if the fight itself isn't a difficult enough feat, you go out there and make each other hurt until one of you is hurt so much less than the other that he leaves the winner. Whoever is less hurt, they win. The goal is to minimize your pain, maximize your opponent's pain, and force the other person to quit. But no one leaves the fight without a scratch.

Worst-case outcome is that you permanently put a loss on your record. That's a risk every fighter takes when they step into the cage. Not only would a loss mean a permanent stain on your record, it also means you got beat up in front of a hundred thousand people to the point where you were more hurt than your opponent. It means your opponent got the best of you in front of an audience. I retract what I said about embarrassment, because a loss is humiliating. Even if you put up a good fight, it's still humiliating.

Never mind the fact that you just got your butt kicked; it's a whole new level of feeling failure in front of a crowd. It's like being a little kid, standing up in the middle of class, and somebody pulls your pants down. It's hard. It's crushing. It can absolutely destroy you. But it's just a loss, and losses happen.

Bethany

In the fall of 2015, I traveled to Antalya, Turkey, to compete in the United World Wrestling Submission Grappling Tournament. After the competition, I decided to take advantage of being overseas by going to visit one of my best friends, who lived just outside of Paris. In the world of martial arts, you are never buddy-buddy with anyone before competing. Afterwards, however, a shared love and passion for the sport turns competitors into comrades, and fighters are generally friendly with the exception of those who have a particularly strong rivalry.

During my layover en route to Paris, I ran into some of the members of the French grappling team who were heading home from the same tournament. We made formal introductions, and they invited me to join them for lunch. One tolerable airport meal and a great conversation later, we all rushed to catch our respective flights.

I arrived in Paris at 4 p.m. and ran into one of the guys again in the baggage claim area. Competing never allows me to travel light, and he must have noticed that I was a bit weighed down by all my luggage. He asked where I was going and checked if I needed help. Even though I had plenty of time to make the 8 p.m. train, I gratefully accepted his offer to help map my train schedule and get me to my first stop, the Metro station.

With my new friend's help, I made it to the correct station with plenty of time to spare, so I pulled my phone out of my bag and started texting my mom to let her know I had arrived safely.

While I was typing, the Metro car arrived. As a crowd of people exited the train car, I stuffed my phone away and joined the crush of passengers making their way on the train, toting my luggage behind me. Once settled, I went to finish the text, but my phone was gone. I dug through my bag frantically, but it was nowhere to be found.

An intense fear threatened to overtake me. As I left the Metro and made my way toward the train station, it no longer mattered that I was a professional mixed martial artist, or that just forty-eight hours earlier I had held my own in a world championship. There I was in Paris, by myself, with a bunch of luggage, trying not to panic because I did not speak the language. I could no longer rely on my phone's GPS function to guide me, and I had no way to communicate with my friend who was waiting for me and who I had been texting all day up until that point. I felt panic rising in my gut, but I knew I could not let fear defeat me.

A crucial part of training for a competition is developing mental toughness. Stepping into a ring to face off with another fighter requires focus of the most intense kind. Victory is won or lost by a series of split decisions. There is no time for second guessing. You are trained to identify quickly any opportunity to take down your opponent, and to act with confidence and precision. You are also in a constant state of analyzing and addressing your own vulnerabilities.

The training I had undergone for the grappling tournament also applied on the streets of Paris. I was at a disadvantage, but I had my train ticket and a general map of which train I needed to get on. It would have to be enough. I took one deep breath after another, and with focused attention to road signs and city maps I managed to find the right train station. I boarded my train with only five minutes to spare.

Once I was safely in my seat, all the stress and anxiety surrounding the competition, traveling, culture shock, and navigating my way through the day burst through my defenses. I broke down.

On the flip side of mental toughness is emotional decompression. Only after the fight do you have the distance necessary to appreciate and analyze what you just experienced, what you could have done differently, and what you will do next time if a similar situation presents itself. While I was still fighting against fear to find the train station, I kept repeating to myself, "You can't freak out. You can't freak out. You can't freak out. You need to find where you're supposed to go." I knew that giving into panic would not improve my situation. But once I was where I needed to be, I was no longer afraid, and it was safe to acknowledge the intensity of what I had just gone through. With that acknowledgment came waves of relief and gratitude.

Mental toughness for me is embodied in certain times, in isolated incidents—but it is not necessarily embedded deep within our culture or even necessarily in our daily lives. There are times when it is important for me to stay calm, focused, and vigilant, but I always do so with the intent of reaching a safe space where I can let my guard down. Emotions can only be kept at bay for so long.

When I finally get to that safe place, I can let everything I've been suppressing come to the surface. I had been pushing myself to the limits for an extended period of time. Losing my phone was just the breaking point for me after months of hard training followed by an intense week of weight cut, and of course general travel anxiety and competition anxiety that left me feeling disoriented. In that moment, my phone was functioning as a lifeline, connecting me to loved ones and allowing me to easily navigate my unfamiliar surroundings. Feeling unraveled and afraid by the unexpected loss of that resource was completely natural, and there is no shame in having those feelings. At the same time, the entire experience affirmed for me the value of cultivating mental toughness, not only for when I step into the ring, but in all aspects of life.

Engaging Mental Toughness Every Day

Reflect on a time when you let your mind get the better of you. How would you approach that situation differently today, recognizing that you have control over your mind?

_____

_____

_____

_____

_____

_____

_____

_____

_____

_____

_____

_____

_____

_____

_____

_____

_____

_____

_____

_____

_____

_____

EMBRACING TEAMWORK

Coming together is a beginning;
keeping together is progress;
working together is success.
—Henry Ford

What Does Embracing Teamwork Mean to Team KO?

Teamwork means that you work together to create a strategy that utilizes each member's respective strengths to the team's advantage. It means sharing responsibility equally among team members and relinquishing individual control. No man is left behind.

Team KO

When we decided to audition for *Spartan: Ultimate Team Challenge* in August 2015, it's not like the four of us were total strangers. But when you don't know someone well, you don't try to drag all the specifics of their life and story out of them. You don't press for details when they share bits and pieces. For the audition videos, however, we had to get deep, and because of that the auditioning process ended up being the foundation for our teamwork.

Making our audition videos was the first time all four of us really got personal with each other. It was kind of a weird way to start things because we had to share with each other things you don't normally share with a lot of people, but it was good for our team. We explored all the highlights and lowlights of each of our lives and got to know each other on a whole other level.

So, after spilling our life stories to each other, what's left? What is there to be uncomfortable about?

Hearing the stories from start to finish, and getting to know each other as deeply and quickly as we did, made all the pieces fit well together. Suddenly our intense motivation and passion for what we do made sense, and we felt like we'd known each other for years. That bond keeps us close.

Zac

During *Spartan: Ultimate Team Challenge,* the girls were just stepping all over Andres's head as we went over the slip wall. Granted, we told them ahead of time not to worry about asking if anything hurt, but they took us up on that way more than we expected. It was funny because ahead of time they said, "No, we don't want to step on your head. We can step on your shoulders instead." Come race day, though, we get there and the first thing they do is *BAM*—foot on the head.

Truthfully, I think we all expected most of the obstacles to be a piece of cake, but we get to the first wall obstacle on the show, not even the dreaded slip wall, and we all just sort of paused for a second. You couldn't reach the top of it on your own, and they designed it like that purposefully. The obstacles on the show were not all obstacles that you could ever feasibly do on your own. In fact, there were some obstacles that all five members *had* to be a part of to move on, like the rope climb. All five members had to be on the rope at the same time, and then there was a flag in the water that had to be passed up to the highest member, who hooked it at the top of the rope. Only once the flag had been hooked could everyone climb down and move on.

Thankfully, we worked well together on that obstacle. Bethany was the anchor at the bottom and did her job well, keeping the rope where it needed to be. We had Andres go up first, and we planned it that way before we even started. Rope is also Jess's strength, but we had Andres shimmy up first because he would have to hold on the longest. And then I also could climb quickly and hold on for a while, which left a shorter distance for the girls to have to climb. We strategized based on everyone's strength and usually had guys go first for an obstacle that used a lot of strength or needed a base.

There was also a log swing obstacle where Andres had to do this sweet Tarzan entrance during our second time through the race. All of us had to get on the log, and on the other side of the water was an inflatable landing. The idea was for all of us to get on the log, rock it back and forth to get momentum, and then jump to the landing one by one.

But if you missed the landing and fell into the water, you had to stay there until everyone else made it off the log. It sucked. And the water is real cold in December, so even just sitting in the water takes energy.

That second time around, we already knew our original plan wasn't going to work. We put the girls on the log and gave it two or three good pushes to get the momentum we couldn't get when we were already on the log.

We pushed it twice, and we said we were going to push it once more before Andres jumped on, and then I was supposed to jump the next time it swung back. But whenever the log swung back, it didn't stay very long. Andres couldn't jump on easily quite like he pictured, so he somehow grabbed the side of the log, like one of the ropes, and swung sideways onto it. It was the coolest thing! He looked like some sort of cartoon character.

As far as working together as a team, throwing a fifth person into the mix so last minute—the Spartan elite—was like throwing in a last-minute, unpredictable variable. We didn't know what to expect. The obstacles were team based and took a lot of energy, and it pushed us all to a point of breaking down mentally. That's hard for a lot of people to handle. Once something gets challenging and attacks you mentally, a lot of people are just done. We carried those methods and ways of thinking with us into the show.

And here's the other thing about competing with a team, even one as close as ours. You can do everything flawlessly, but one person being off their game affects everyone's results. When you compete as a team, you give up control to some extent. It's a hard thing to do, recognizing that it's not all in your power. In a fight, there is no one else to blame when you don't win. In the show, as in any team race or sport, you can so easily fall into blaming others. It's hard to play as a team, but it pays off in the end.

Andres

On April 30, 2016, Jess and I ran the Spartan Ultra Beast on the premise of being in it together—as a team. We said that we were going to start the race together and finish the race together, and that's exactly what we did.

Within the first two or three miles of that thirty-mile race, Jess failed an obstacle. And, of course, every time you fail an obstacle, you have to do thirty burpees (a combination of a push-up, squat, and jump—Google it) as your penalty. She starts doing her burpees, and I'm standing and waiting.

Now, one thing you need to know about Jessica is that she *hates* doing burpees. You can see it all over her face. She seems to take the burpees as a personal insult against her progress. I mean, everyone hates doing burpees, but starting a race as long as the Ultra Beast with burpees is particularly rough. It can really mess with your head.

"If you want to go ahead, just go. Just go," Jess insisted.

"Yeah, I'm about to go. Finish your burpees first," I said. We were only two or three miles into this race, and I didn't come just to do it by myself. I was there as part of a team.

"Just go."

"Yeah, I'm about to go. As soon as you finish your burpees."

She finally finished her burpees, and we ran on. For the first half of the race, I was the one keeping up the pace. Jess was dealing with an upset stomach, so I had to be the one pushing us. When we took off from the midway point break, she was feeling better, and I was okay at first, but after a few more miles of pounding down hills, my knees were done. They were hurting. Jess had to take over the role of pushing our pace, and I was just trying to keep up once she finally got going.

Keep running. Keep moving. Stay with your team.

The point is, the whole time we motivated each other, stayed together, and finished the race together. It's always been like that with her, and with Bethany and Zac too for the show. I've had races where I was just going to race and go after my fastest time, but if you are going to run as a team, it needs to be about the team.

Understand that in a team, not everybody's the same. People have strengths and weaknesses that are different from the person next to them. You have to know that going in and consider that one of your teammates might be weaker or might fail at something. It might slow you down, but you went into it as a team. In some cases, you might be the one slowing everyone else down. Personal bests have to be pushed aside to support your teammates. When they're at their breaking point, when they miss an obstacle and have to do burpees, when they're pissed off, tired, or walking because their legs hurt, you're there to push them and help them get better. Finish the race with the person you started with.

At an earlier Wintergreen race, I did the same thing with our team's friend Buck Grant—really, he's more like an extension of Team KO— who is a martial arts coach and obstacle course racer. This was the second time I had raced the Wintergreen course, but Buck was newer to racing. It's a trying course, and we were racing up a hill when his legs cramped and he fell to the ground. He couldn't get up. Like Jessica at the Ultra Beast, he told me to keep going without him. But we were doing the race together.

There was no way I was going to leave him. Buck had electrolyte tubes in his pack, and I kept telling him to take them. He acknowledged everything I said but didn't make a move—he was really struggling—so we stayed put for a good fifteen minutes before I dug his electrolytes and gel pack out of his bag and gave them to him so we could continue the race.

What's cool about Buck is that he comes to the table with years of coaching experience. He's been an athlete himself and has coached other athletes, but this was a whole different ball game for him like it had been for me. We had the same comradery that Jess and I had. Jessica was able to help me through that learning process, and then I was able to help Buck. We started together and finished together—as a team.

Embracing Teamwork Every Day

You may have to give up some level of control when you work with a team. It's not easy, but it's worth it. Think of a team you work with. Can you identify each member's biggest strength? Can you identify one area of weakness that you can improve to better compliment the team?

_____

_____

_____

_____

_____

_____

_____

_____

_____

_____

_____

_____

_____

_____

_____

_____

_____

_____

_____

_____

WELCOMING THE UNKNOWN

*Don't let the fear of the unknown keep you from
experiencing a life greater than you have ever known.*
—Jeff McClung

What Does Welcoming the Unknown Mean to Team KO?

You face unpredictability and the unknown every day, whether you
want to or not. Welcoming the unknown means taking advantage of
opportunities in front of you, even when you don't know what the
outcome will be. It doesn't mean jumping blindly without a plan,
but it does mean being okay with the unpredictable circumstances of
everyday life.

Andres

When my family and I moved to Colombia the year I turned nine, I started a new school in a new country. One of my biggest challenges was my education, and school in Colombia was completely different from what I'd gotten used to in the States. School in Colombia wasn't as sophisticated as school in the States, although I was introduced to wearing uniforms, and everyone was reading and writing in Spanish. I didn't know the language that well, so I learned as I went. The school was just buildings and classrooms, like most schools, and outside everything was just sparse grass and dirt. But there was always a soccer field.

A few weeks after the move, my grandma passed away. She was already in the hospital when we arrived in the country. Her death was hard on the whole family. I was only nine years old, and the closest I'd ever been to her was talking on the phone.

The first couple of years in Colombia were fine. We lived with extended family at first, but after about a year everyone went their separate ways. My family moved around a lot for financial reasons, so everything was always changing, and I constantly had to adjust.

When I moved back to the States, I was fifteen and made the trip alone. It meant having to adjust again, and I didn't start high school right away because I came in the middle of the school year. After speaking primarily Spanish in Colombia for so long, it was hard for me to go back to speaking English all the time. Slowly, the language came back, but it took a lot of work. When I finally started my freshman year of high school, I was awarded honors every marking period, so academically I was able to keep up.

Despite my good grades, when it came to college I had no idea what it was all about. I never did anything to prepare myself. I didn't know what sort of career I wanted, what I wanted to study, or anything like that. Adjusting to new countries and cultures growing up took a lot of my focus all through high school, and I could really only see as far as graduation. I got to my senior year and had no clue what I was going to do afterwards. I had so many questions and uncertainties about college that the military emerged as an appealing, clear-cut option for me.

In 2008, I graduated high school and left for boot camp a month or two later. I'd always admired the military and the ideal of discipline, and I ended up visiting the Navy recruiter when the military first piqued my interest. Intrigued by his description of the SEAL program, I decided to go the Navy route.

Once I was decided, I spent the rest of my senior year working toward that goal and training for it physically, including swimming. When I got to boot camp, it didn't quite live up to my expectations. It was less than I expected. I had an image in my head of what boot camp would be like that came mostly from TV. I'd seen shows and movies where they trained hard, and if one person did something wrong, everyone had to drop and give the drill instructor twenty. It looked crazy intense, and that excited me. But when I got there, it was nothing like that.

Although the physical challenge may have been lacking, boot camp was yet another foreign environment I had to adjust to. It was the first time I had been away from all my family. It was isolating. When you're there, you have no idea what is happening in the outside world. Even if you don't normally pay attention to the outside world, not being *able* to watch the news and keep up with current events feels quite different. You take for granted seeing or hearing about things like that online or on TV. All of that was taken away. Nothing exists outside of that base.

That isolation gives you a lot of time to think. You start reflecting on your life: who you are, what you've done, who you want to become, the decisions you've made, the decisions you will make, your family, etc.

It gets lonely.

At ten every night, we were all supposed to go to sleep. But once the instructors left for the night, we were like little kids. Everybody climbed out of their racks, and we would just talk, getting to know each other, asking about where the others were from and about their families. We all saw the need for social interaction after so little time being isolated. It was hard to be alone in that unknown. It was hard every single day. I'd write letters to my family about everything, good and bad.

The mental toughness took a lot of thinking, getting in touch with myself, and bracing myself for whatever came next.

Bethany

I grew up with a large family—three sisters and three brothers. Things were always a bit unpredictable in our household. I was conditioned from the start to go with the flow and not always abide by a plan. My parents had a lot on their plate, so we learned to be flexible as kids. As a family, we were taught to be team players even though sometimes there was so much happening we didn't know exactly what was going on. I learned very early that trying to fight the unknown is much less effective than welcoming it.

That conditioning has helped me profoundly. So many people feel the need to have a specific plan, a specific goal, and outlined action steps to get there, and a lot of times in life things don't go according to plan. You have to be okay with the realization that you could have a flawless plan and everything could still fall apart. You have to be okay with the fact that you don't always know exactly how some things will play out.

For example, when NBC chose us to be competitors on *Ultimate Team Challenge*, we didn't know exactly what the show was going to be like. It was the first season. We certainly speculated about what the experience would be like, but we were going into it blindly. When you're approaching a situation like that, I think it's most important individually to recognize that there will be curveballs thrown at you and things you don't know how to tackle, but you have to face them head-on anyway and give 100 percent effort. Being able to think on my feet is essential in everything I do, from fighting—where you have to react immediately— to racing to being on *Ultimate Team Challenge*. You never know what will come at you. The only things we can control are the actions we take and the reactions to what comes at us.

If your mind is in the right place and you picture your goal and stay focused on that goal, everything unknown that is thrown at you is just an obstacle that must be figured out. I don't think there's anything that can't be figured out if you put your mind to it, decide to take a leap, and just go for it. Anything worth doing will have a certain amount of risk and uncertainty. For my mentor, David Hancock, that is the very definition of entrepreneurship: being willing to take a risk for potential gain.

So I've always applied that philosophy no matter what I'm doing. To achieve any kind of greatness or anything of excellence, you have to be able to take those risks and jump in with both feet, even if you don't know what the outcome will look like. People lose out on opportunities because they don't like not being able to see where they will land. They want everything perfectly planned out, and sometimes by that time it's too late.

Coming to terms with not completing something the way you want to is far less disappointing than never trying at all.

I know that sounds cliché, but a lot of times you just don't know how an opportunity will unfold. However, being okay with that unknown is a million times better than the guilt or the disappointment of not even trying. It all boils down to your own actions and reactions, the only things you can control. Having a plan is good, but you can't count on things always going according to plan, and you have to be prepared and open when that happens.

Welcoming the Unknown Every Day

Take a chance and be okay with not being able to see the end result clearly just yet. Think of a current opportunity that you haven't pulled the trigger on. What is holding you back? Is that worth missing the opportunity?

_____

_____

_____

_____

_____

_____

_____

_____

_____

_____

_____

_____

_____

_____

_____

_____

_____

_____

_____

_____

_____

WAKING UP WITH DETERMINATION

*Failure will never overtake me if my
determination to succeed is strong enough.*
—**Og Mandino**

What Does Waking Up with Determination Mean
to Team KO?

Waking up with determination means you approach your goals with
unwavering resolution every single day. It means maintaining a firmness
of purpose and unrelenting drive in pursuit of your goals—consistently
putting one foot in front of the other, despite inevitable weariness.

Andres

Around the age of fourteen, shortly before moving back to the States, I decided to start working out.

I honestly don't know what prompted that decision, but I was really into the idea of lifting. It made me feel strong, and I craved that strength. I decided to do one hundred pushups and one hundred sit-ups every single day. I don't know where that goal came from, or what triggered me to start working out every day, but from that day on I was incredibly disciplined.

It got to the point where if I went one day without working out, either from laziness or forgetfulness, I would make up for it the next day and complete two hundred pushups and two hundred sit-ups. If I skipped a whole week, the first day I was back at it I would have to make up for all seven days: seven hundred pushups and seven hundred sit-ups.

Once I got into that, I decided to make my own dumbbell by taking cement mix and putting it in some kitchen Tupperware that my mom had (pretty creative, if I do say so myself). I found two Tupperware containers the same size, got the cement mix, put it in there, got a pipe, and put that in there. I added some of the mix inside the pipe to make it stronger and let it dry. Once it had dried, I flipped it over and did the other side of the dumbbell the same way.

After my dumbbell was made, I only did curls.

At the time, I didn't know any details about working out. I did the exercise that I saw the most on TV. So every time I worked out, I only did bicep curls. In my mind, that was somehow working out my whole body. I didn't know about the biceps, the triceps, the quadriceps, etc. I just imagined the body as one big muscle, and this one exercise was going to work that giant muscle.

But I kept at it.

Bethany

Growing up, I knew that one day I wanted to own my own business. The opportunity just happened to come into my life much earlier than expected.

The gym where I trained for years was more than just a gym. It was my second home. And the community of fighters who got together and trained was my second family. When Zac was sick, the gym hosted a fundraiser in his honor and supported my decision to take a step back from training to take care of Zac.

After two years of putting the gym and fighting on the back burner, I finally came back, only to discover that the gym that shaped me had spiraled downhill. A lack of administrative support had done serious damage to the operational side of the gym, and my coach, who owned the gym at the time, confided in me that he could not do it anymore. That hit me hard. In just a couple of years the gym had gone from being a safe space that stood steady through some of my biggest personal trials to being an almost nonexistent state, and it was going to close unless something changed. I asked what needed to be done to keep the gym operational. The only way the gym would make it was if someone came on as an owner to get the administrative side of the business back on track.

I did a mental assessment of everyone involved at the gym and figured that the only person with the flexibility, experience, and determination needed to save the gym was me. A few days later my name was added to the lease, and at twenty-four years old I was the new owner of a ship that was quickly going under.

Although I had a good idea of what it was going to take to be an owner of the gym, my first days hit me hard. Our rent was due right away, and we didn't have it. It might come as a surprise that, despite being a professional fighter, I am not a confrontational person. But that first week I drove door to door to each fighter's home and collected the money for their training. I made a deposit just in time to deliver our check to the landlord on time.

I wish I could say it was smooth sailing from that point on, but there was an obstacle around every corner that seemed designed to challenge my determination to get the gym fully functional and sustainable.

One of the many obstacles that came up early on was when the guy we were borrowing our wrestling mats from needed them back right away. We had the mats on indefinite loan from a wrestling club that had dissolved. Out of the blue, the guy who loaned them to us gave us notice that he had promised the mats to another wrestling club and would be by the next day to pick them up. The only piece of equipment I needed to run my business was getting ripped out from under me, and I had to act quickly. I had students coming the next week to train and knew we would have to be creative for a couple of practices. By some miracle, I found mats at a reasonable price in Maryland and put my own money down on them. I rented a U-Haul, drove to pick them up, and had them on the gym floor by the end of that week.

With each new obstacle came the same old question: how badly do you want this?

For me, that answer was easy. The gym was not just business. It was personal.

I started training for MMA when I was sixteen, at the age when many young women are trying to figure out who they are as individuals. MMA gave me an avenue to be a competitive athlete, to really test and challenge myself. It provided an opportunity for me to overcome my paralyzing shyness by being a safe space for me to leave my comfort zone and deepen my self-confidence. It was where I went to relieve stress and re-center myself when life became overwhelming. Of course, the gym was more than just a space—it wasn't the location we were at or the equipment we had, it was the core group of people who were there with me when I was fighting to find my own place in this world.

What we had as a team was special. What we had gave me a reason every single day to put just about everything on the line to make sure our community would not only survive but thrive.

I can't tell you what drives people's determination, and not everyone has the same passion for whatever it is they do, but for me that passion is what drove it—the community and the family I had there. Optimism alone was not enough to keep me motivated when every day, every little decision mattered. The business was so fragile that any little thing could make or break it, but I needed it to stay open. I was willing to keep on going no matter what, rather than give that up. I managed to turn setbacks into opportunities for growth.

Unless you feel the pain and resistance as you move toward your goals, you will not leave your comfort zone. Until you're ready to fight through setbacks and break boundaries, you will not grow. I would not have been able to break those boundaries on my own unless those challenging situations were forced upon me. I had to overcome them. All those things that should have been deal breakers were overcome only because I continued to fight them, put the blinders on, and focused on what was in front of me, day after day, until that forward momentum came around again.

Waking Up with Determination Every Day

You want to reach your goal for a reason, and staying determined through setbacks is key. Write down a mantra that you can repeat to yourself when weariness tells you to quit. Keep it somewhere you can see every morning.

_____

_____

_____

_____

_____

_____

_____

_____

_____

_____

_____

_____

_____

_____

_____

_____

_____

_____

_____

_____

COMMUNICATING WITH CLARITY

The greatest gifts you can give your team: clarity, communication, and pulling people together around a shared mission.
—**Anne Sweeney**

What Does Communicating with Clarity Mean to Team KO?

Communicating with clarity means making an effort to deliver constructive criticism openly and directly with good intentions. At the same time, it means listening to constructive criticism with the intention of receiving and understanding the core meaning of what someone else is saying without getting defensive.

Zac

Over time, three areas of communication have revealed themselves to be most important to me, and I have decided to make sure they are a part of how I communicate with others around me: honesty, listening, and confirmation.

One area where I see miscommunication pop up all the time is when people let a fear of being wrong, or a fear of exposing that they don't know something, get in the way of clear communication and progress. Not being honest about these things can wreak havoc on communication and hinder all sorts of progress. People don't want to be wrong. For some reason, it destroys them. It makes them feel like they made a mistake. For some reason, saying *I'm wrong* or *I didn't know that* is something they can't handle, and it usually results in hazy communication.

Being honest is inconvenient. Honesty often results in difficult conversations. But being honest is playing the long game, while being dishonest, especially on a white lie level, shows zero forethought and is playing the short game.

By choosing to be honest on every level, you choose to play the long game. You know that you are doing yourself a service by ensuring you don't have future stresses to bear due to the consequences of your seemingly harmless white lies. Don't let the fear of being wrong take away your ability to play the long game. Be honest with those around you.

Honesty with others is important, but just as important is being honest with yourself.

That's what will really pay off in the long game. If you are truly honest with yourself, you should be able to get ahead of any long-term problems. Strive to be objective in how you view yourself, as this can lead to great insight and self-awareness. And if you're not, it becomes easy to take on a victim mentality and blame the circumstances, rather than the actions *you* took that led to those circumstances.

Another crucial part of communication is listening. Challenging how you receive information and how you react to the events around you are necessary steps in creating an environment for complete clarity. To communicate effectively, you must be able to receive information for what it is—information—without attaching a bias or taking it personally. That can be challenging, but it is a vital part of clear communication and allows room for others to be forthright without feeling like they have to walk on eggshells lest they get a negative response.

The third area of communication that stands out for me is confirmation. You can never be too clear. And you can't be clear at all if you don't have some sort of confirmation from everyone involved that they have heard and understood you.

A good team will accept your communication for what it is: communicating for the benefit of the common goal. A good team will listen to what is being communicated and respond in a way that ensures quick clarity. A good teammate will express that they are on board, and that they understand or agree/disagree for whatever reason. It should be an even exchange. The goal of all team members should be making sure there are no gray areas, and that everyone is on board with striving for clarity in all communication.

Team KO

From the get-go, we agreed not to take offense at anything said while we all trained together for *Ultimate Team Challenge*. We were all on the same page. We didn't want to let little things become big things, like getting wrapped up in the way someone phrased a criticism or amendment to our game plan. We were all trying to get important points across, so it was about making sure we got to those points without getting distracted by the way we delivered them, especially since we all have different communication styles. But we all had the same goal: win the show.

We decided to weed through the parts of what someone else said that we didn't understand or that rubbed us the wrong way to comprehend the core of what each of us was trying to communicate at any given time. We each made an effort to understand and not nit-pick about tone or wording—even when we had differing views, which we often did as this was the first time the four of us had competed together.

When it came to the four of us competing and racing together, we had no preexisting problems, but we had also never been in an environment with so much pressure before. And, for the show, the obstacles required working together as a team.

Even during the moments when we were bumping heads or heading in that direction, we consciously made the effort to work together: no one tried to be the loudest or have the biggest voice and rule over the others. We had each other's backs and were able to adapt. There was no time for beating around the bush, so we all just had to be straightforward.

There was no time to worry about playing nice. We weren't mean, but we did have to tell each other what we meant without fluffing it up. This was hard. It's natural to want everyone to understand the reasons behind the things we say, but for the sake of time and clarity, we had to adjust.

Even after training for the race, communication still got jumbled once we were actually on the show. We had some tricky situations where it was hard to keep in mind the agreement we'd reached before competing, but overall, laying out the ground rules for communication ahead of time really helped us.

Communicating with Clarity Every Day

Communication is a two-way street, and at any point you could be delivering or receiving. Don't let the little things—like the way something is worded—get in the way of communicating things that need to be known and understood. Think of a person with whom communication is particularly challenging. Is it because of the topic or the methods of delivery and reception? What can you do to make sure that your method of communication prioritizes the topic?

_____

_____

_____

_____

_____

_____

_____

_____

_____

_____

_____

_____

_____

_____

_____

_____

_____

_____

AVOIDING NEGATIVE COMPARISON

We won't be distracted by comparison
if we are captivated with purpose.
—Bob Goff

What Does Avoiding Negative Comparison Mean to Team KO?

Comparison is looking at someone else or a past version of yourself and seeing how you measure up, both in healthy and unhealthy ways. It is a good way to identify where we want to be and how far we've come, but should never be taken as an indication of failure or success. Comparison can be a healthy motivator, but we must be mindful not to let the comparison itself become all-consuming and get in the way of our goals.

Bethany

Often as we are reaching toward our goals, we encounter others who have the same goals. It's important that when we do, we don't conduct negative comparisons in our minds.

Comparison can be a healthy tool when used well, but it can also be very damaging if not kept in check.

On the healthy side, comparison helps keep us accurate in our self-evaluation and progress. It can lead to self-reflection as we observe the efforts and results of others, or learn as we watch the methods of others. Comparison is, and should be, a prevalent part of any competition. Without comparison, there is no competition. Competition provides a healthy platform for comparison with necessary and precise parameters. If used wisely, that comparison can lead to greater personal progress. But while comparison can lead to a higher level of motivation, it should never be the drive behind it.

At what point does comparison become unhealthy on an individual level?

The line between healthy and unhealthy comparison gets crossed when you don't set appropriate boundaries in your mind for the comparison between yourself and others.

Comparing your journey to another's and being jealous or judgmental is not a fruitful use of time. Neither is looking at yourself either poorly or highly because of comparison. Control the parameters of your comparison to meet the parameters of the competition.

At what point does the comparison take a personal turn? At that point, it's important to reroute your thoughts.

Remember that it doesn't always come down to you or somebody else. There can be room for many people to shine, and there's no reason to feel like you're less successful than another or that you can't accomplish your goals just because someone else is accomplishing theirs.

When you transition from looking at everyone as a competitor, you start asking yourself how you can see them in a different light and work *with* them toward the bigger picture of what you're all trying to accomplish. That's not always practical in highly competitive situations (for example, if you're going into the cage against someone in an MMA fight, it is your goal versus their goals; you have to win). In those moments, we still need to remember how much we depend on each other to accomplish what we have as a whole.

Jess

2016 was only my second year competing in the elite heats of Spartan races, and when I went up to the starting lines with pro athletes, I asked myself every single time: *why am I here?*

Every single time I race, I question whether I belong.

Everyone always says not to compare yourself to other racers, but that's the first thing I do. I start thinking that I can't keep up. When the B*tch gets in your head and you start comparing yourself to other competitors, it's telling you that you're not good enough. That's the unhealthy part of comparison—allowing the comparison to create feelings of inadequacy, feeling like you will never be on the same level as someone else, and eventually quitting.

Now, comparison can also certainly be a healthy part of competition. If you're comparing yourself to someone at the gym or in a race in a way that challenges you to try to surpass that person or be better at what you're doing, it can be good for you competitively. But a lot of the time, comparison gets in your head instead and makes you doubt your abilities.

One race where I had to fight the B*tch harder than usual on comparison was the 2015 Spartan World Championship race. Even though I had earned my coin all the way back in May, I didn't find out until two days before I was supposed to run in October.

I never thought I would be one of those women to be a coin holder. *Never.*

Being a coin holder, going into something that big, was a dream I never thought would come true. The championship was the race everyone had been training for, and being in the coin-holder elite class for it seemed unreal. (There are four different ways you can become a coin holder, but I earned mine by placing high enough in the elite heat of a particular race. It meant that I was one of only five hundred slots Spartan fills with athletes from all over the world.)

It's funny because I was actually invited to train in Mammoth Lakes with another athlete and her coach to prepare for the elevation of the championship race. I was there three weeks prior to the world championship, fighting the B*tch the whole time as I trained beside two pro athletes who knew they had earned their coin. I had no idea that I was also a coin holder, and as I was out there training on the mountain, I kept wondering what I was doing there. *What did I think I was doing training with these coin holders?* At the time, I just knew it was something I had to do.

Going into the championship, I knew I was standing among the coin holders for a reason. I belonged. I had earned it. But even holding that coin didn't mean I wasn't fighting the B*tch every step of the race.

That's the unhealthy side of comparison. Incorporating comparison in a healthy way means being able to recognize that the B*tch is there. Know that you have to keep going anyway. You have to ignore the B*tch because everyone else lined up with you, even the pros, have that same B*tch. Do what you have to do. Keep going.

You just might discover that you measure up after all.

Avoiding Negative Comparison Every Day

While it can be motivational to compete with others, using their progress as an indication of your own is unhealthy. Keep in mind that you may very well be comparing your beginning to someone else's middle. Without comparing yourself to anyone, think of one milestone that you've achieved in the past month. How do you feel about it? Is it progress from where you were before? Repeat this exercise whenever you find yourself looking at your accomplishments as less than others'.

ACKNOWLEDGING LEADERSHIP

Great leaders don't set out to be a leader... they set out to make a difference. It's never about the role—always about the goal.
—Lisa Haisha

What Does Acknowledging Leadership Mean to Team KO?

Leadership means taking on the role of leader when you need to, but also recognizing when someone else can better fill that role and it's your turn to follow. When you surround yourself with teammates whose strengths complement and balance your own weaknesses, the leadership role will naturally change hands depending on the circumstances. Communication, accountability, and respect for the current leadership role are crucial in these transitions.

Team KO

During *Spartan: Ultimate Team Challenge*, the NBC crew kept asking us, "Who's your team leader?"

Technically, Katie (our NBC-assigned fifth team member) was intended to be our team captain. The truth is—and this is the answer we gave them every time—we all have different strengths that allow us to lead at different times. Whoever was in front of the pack and needed to take on the role was the one who led. Part of being a good team member is knowing when to let someone else take the lead. We did bump heads sometimes, but we were under a tremendous amount of pressure. We did pretty well, all things considered. And we were excited. I'm sure we could have been a little more organized, but it worked out.

One obstacle where leadership shifted among all of us evenly was when we had to run through water with shields. The person in front changed often, depending on who had the strength and motivation to set the pace in that moment. At one point it was the guys in front, and then Jess and Bethany took over before handing it over to Katie for a bit.

We also planned for how we would work together as a team for certain obstacles such as the log lift. We did shift things around during the race, but they were changes we had decided on ahead of time in between our two races. Everyone was synchronized because we were all on the same page. None of us tried to do something different unless everyone was already aware, and that's what kept us moving quickly and working together.

Acknowledging Leadership Every Day

Know when to lead, but also know when it's someone else's turn to take that role. It takes cooperation from everyone on the team to support the leadership role. Think of a team that you work with, and identify times in your team's process when you are not the active leader. Knowing your skill set, how can you best support the active leader during those times?

_____

_____

_____

_____

_____

_____

_____

_____

_____

_____

_____

_____

_____

_____

_____

_____

_____

_____

_____

ADOPTING A PREPARED MINDSET

By failing to prepare, you are preparing to fail.
—**Benjamin Franklin**

What Does Adopting a Prepared Mindset Mean to Team KO?

Adopting a prepared mindset means identifying your knowledge gaps and then creating a step-by-step plan to fill those gaps and accomplish your goal. It is making sure you are ready to take action, while also working balance and rest into your plan to avoid burnout.

Andres

When you're approaching a fight, you want to be at your absolute best.

Now, being at your best is not easy, and you can't be at your best 24/7. So you train year round, you stay active, you learn new techniques, but when it comes to your eight- to ten-week fight camp, training becomes your primary focus and your top priority. Everything else comes second.

There is no wimping out of training during fight camp; you give 110 percent every day for that time period. You're going for your best cardio, your best strength training, your best conditioning, and you're trying to get to the point where you can throw your fastest and strongest punch, have the fastest reaction time, etc. You have to be so focused that all else is put aside. The fight is your goal—your only goal.

When you're not in fight camp, it's not like that. You can train one day, and then maybe the next there's something more important you need to get done, or you're not feeling good and take it easy. During fight camp, you can't afford that. If you take days off, you'll end up losing because somewhere out there, your opponent is training to beat you up. That's the name of the game.

You are training to go into a cage and fight somebody, somebody who is also training to punch you. Hard. And hurt you. That's how they're going to win. So you have to be training to stop them and do the same damage and more back to them. The pressure is intense.

Outside of fight camp, a bad day is no big deal.

In fight camp, you know the target ahead of you. If you have a bad day, it affects your mental game. You can't throw combos right, you keep tripping. Whatever it is, you start worrying that it will happen in the fight, picturing your opponent getting the best of you. Those negative thoughts can hold you back and weigh you down, and it affects your confidence levels.

You never want to go into a fight with low confidence, feeling like you're not ready, like the other guy is better than you, like there's nothing you can do to beat him.

You are there to win. That is your goal—to push yourself as far as you can, mind and body, and react to whatever your opponent throws at you.

Besides a bad day at training, a multitude of other things can affect your overall preparation: your social life, personal life, relationships, kids to worry about, sick family members, stressful work, etc. Really anything can affect it. You might get out of work already tired. But you have to train anyway. You have to learn. You have to fight.

What makes fight camp even harder is cutting weight. Personally, I've never had to cut weight drastically for a fight. I walk around at 165 and fight at 155. It's not a hard weight cut. I'm still able to eat on the day of weigh-ins, which is not something all fighters can say.

Usually fighters are dropping twenty to thirty pounds. They're cutting weight weeks in advance, while I've never had to start earlier than a week before my fight.

When you have to cut twenty or thirty pounds, you have to be a lot stricter. Dieting is a lot more prevalent. When I first had to cut weight, I ate almost nothing but salads. I hate salads. I want steak, chicken, mashed potatoes, all the fat stuff. But something as simple as changing your diet also adds to the stress and pressure of fight camp.

If you're at work and you pull out your three pieces of lettuce, and the person sitting next to you is eating a burger, someone else is munching fries, and another is devouring a burrito, the temptation is off the charts. You can smell their delicious food. You can't smell salad. Lettuce doesn't smell like anything. So self-control becomes key in weight cutting because there is temptation everywhere.

Honestly, choosing food based on what you feel like eating is a regular thing that we all do. You eat what you want, and it's satisfying.

It not only takes your hunger away, it makes you happy. When people are depressed, they eat ice cream because it makes them feel better. So when you have to limit the things you like and eat food you don't really like, it adds stress. You might be craving something, but you can't have it because you have a fight coming. There's a purpose to everything you eat, so you have to stay on track to fuel your body correctly for training.

You get to the day of weigh-ins after eating this healthy diet, and the way most fight diets are designed is in a way that makes it easy to drop a lot of water weight that last day. It's basically dehydration.

Usually fighters will use Epson salt in an extremely hot bath, like so hot that it causes you to sweat. It pulls all the water out of your body, out of your muscles. People say it's a healthier way to lose water weight, but it's still dehydration. I remember getting into the tub, and within ten minutes my whole body was tingling: chest, legs, stomach, everything. When you finally get out of the bath, you're out of breath, which is crazy because you're supposed to go 100 percent against an opponent the next day, and this bath just drained your body of energy.

It can be incredibly frustrating to need to cut those last pounds and weigh in, especially if your tried-and-true methods just aren't working that day. So you do everything at a drastic level and it drains you. There was a time when the Epson salt bath wasn't working for whatever reason, so I asked my roommate to take me to the gym so I could use the sauna. I asked someone else to drive because you can't drive when you're cutting like that—your body is too drained. Going to the sauna, you're trying to lose about ten pounds, so you put on every long-sleeve shirt that you have, sweaters, sweatpants, hoodies, multiple pairs of socks, gloves, whatever you have. I think every fighter has his or her own strategy, but that's mine.

Your body is just a tool for your mind to accomplish whatever it wants, but that does not mean it's comfortable. Your body may be telling you to stop, it doesn't want you to be doing this, but those signals don't indicate your limit. You can keep going, but that's when it takes mental strength to push through those signals. Pain and discomfort make you want to stop. How do you keep going when you know it will continue to cause pain, discomfort, stress you out, and drive you nuts?

We talk about sacrificing for a fight. Beyond the physical preparation, the time that training takes up in your life is huge. When you have a goal like that, something you're working on, the people in your life need to know it's not that you don't care about them or value them. It's that this fight has to be top priority right now. If people are selfish and can't understand the importance of your goal, they have to go. When my fights are coming up, I will not do anything that could possibly sacrifice my potential to win. It's hard because most people don't understand that.

Understanding the intensity and sacrifice involved in training for larger goals is what makes our team special. Not only do we all understand what it takes, but we've also been there, and we all approach a race or challenge that same way. The focus each of us has individually is magnified by the support group of teammates who have the same mindset. That's an unstoppable team.

Of course, there's also the temporary nature of fight camp to consider. Having an end date to all this madness both helps and hurts your mental stamina. It's an insane amount of pressure because you have a limited time to prepare. You wake up in the morning, realize the fight is only three weeks away, and that propels you through the day. But at the end of the day, when you're driving home from practice exhausted and can't even keep your hands on the steering wheel, that time limit becomes a blessing. *I can do this. Only have to survive three more weeks.*

At the end of the day, everything you do is for a purpose. You know what you're doing it for, and you repeat that to yourself. You know those movies that show a football team in the locker room with the coach motivating them before a game? It's kind of like that. Only you're both the coach and the team.

Adopting a Prepared Mindset Every Day

To accomplish a goal, you have to make a detailed plan that includes space for both rest and the unexpected. Identify one goal you have that will require intense preparation. Create a detailed plan for tackling that goal, and identify deadlines on your calendar. How will you balance this preparation with other areas of your life? How will you incorporate rest?

_____

_____

_____

_____

_____

_____

_____

_____

_____

_____

_____

_____

_____

_____

_____

_____

_____

_____

_____

GROWING CONFIDENCE

The way to develop self-confidence is to do the thing you fear and get a record of successful experiences behind you.
—**William Jennings Bryan**

What Does Growing Confidence Mean to Team KO?

Growing confidence comes from repeatedly testing yourself and expanding your boundaries. Confidence does not always come easily or naturally at first, but consistently venturing outside your comfort zone allows that confidence to start growing. By setting smaller, more realistic goals as a starting point, you can ignite your confidence and be ready to tackle increasingly difficult goals.

Zac

You grow confidence by doing, and you grow confidence by controlling your view on failure.

Confidence is not built on your results from just one thing, one single accomplishment. Just the process of trying something new is a big part of gaining or growing confidence. Trying new things, sucking at them a little bit, not being satisfied with that, and refusing to give up—that's what will increase your ability to be confident in whatever the next thing is. And the next thing after that.

So maybe there are a thousand miniature fails in the path toward your end goal. The next time you are working toward a goal, there may only be five hundred miniature fails. Failures must be seen internally as lessons. When you choose to apply those lessons is when your success begins to show, and you gain confidence in your efforts and victories.

Bethany

To be truly confident, you must strive to have a complete understanding of, respect for, and peace with yourself. Confidence requires a lot of honest self-reflection. But the key to confidence is being happy and satisfied with who you are and the choices you've made. Reaching that level of contentment takes a deep look inside. That confidence starts growing when you work to improve yourself, when you work to:

- replace bad habits with positive ones
- challenge your view of thinking on something and expand your understanding
- test yourself in new ways

Sometimes this comes in baby steps. By starting with smaller things and working your way up, you allow yourself the opportunity to accomplish goals with a greater chance of success. As you are successful, or in some cases not successful, in reaching a goal, it's important to take the lessons you learned from that experience and apply them toward the next goal.

Every goal may not be met successfully, but don't let losses or failures stop you from trying again, or cause you to beat yourself up over it, or impact your sense of self-worth. Instead, use the lessons as motivation and fuel for the next goal you set for yourself.

Don't take on things that conflict with your morals, or what in your heart you believe is right for you. Keep your heart and mind engaged when faced with new opportunities, or as you set new goals. Ensure you are doing things that make you feel proud, things that fully resonate with you on your deepest level.

As you make daily choices in alignment with your true intentions, and give yourself the best chance of success with gradual, obtainable goals, your confidence will grow as well as the peace within yourself.

Team KO

The thing about *Ultimate Team Challenge* that was different from any fight was the amount of time we had to prepare and gain confidence in our ability to do well in the races. We didn't have all that long, just long enough to make sure we were in shape. When you're heading into a fight, you really want ten to twelve weeks to get yourself ready. We found out in late October that we had been selected for *Ultimate Team Challenge*, and we were scheduled to film in early December, giving us only five to six weeks to prepare.

The show needed a lot of different things from us. It was like a pro fight in that respect. They needed contracts, paperwork, medicals—a whole lot of stuff. We had to prepare more than just our physical bodies to get ready to compete: we had to arrange travel, fix schedules, get time off work. It was right around the holidays, which was actually nice and made travel somewhat easier.

Even with that preparation, we didn't have confidence in our ability to predict what the show would be like. We had to be okay with the unknown. We spent a lot of time speculating about things as small as team colors. But we found out eventually and were confident going in that the four of us had prepared to the best of our ability. And that's all we could really ask for.

Growing Confidence Every Day

Confidence does not always come innately. Identify a smaller goal within your reach that you can absolutely accomplish, but that still challenges you. Watch as your confidence is boosted afterwards. How will the confidence grown from accomplishing that smaller goal help with larger ones?

_____

_____

_____

_____

_____

_____

_____

_____

_____

_____

_____

_____

_____

_____

_____

_____

_____

_____

_____

_____

BEING RESILIENT

Human beings have enormous resilience.
—Muhammad Yunus

What Does Being Resilient Mean to Team KO?

Resilience is the capacity to keep moving forward, day in and day out, despite extenuating circumstances. It is refusing to be defined by those circumstances and powering through the hard times to emerge a stronger person on the other side.

Andres

After a couple years of living in Colombia as an adolescent, my siblings got older and left, and it was just me and my mom. The struggle got to a point where financially…it was just bad. There were times when my mom couldn't afford to pay the light bill or the water bill, so they would come to the house and shut down the services. We spent days at a time with candles throughout the house because there was no electricity. Sometimes I would have to go with an empty jug to knock on a neighbor's door to ask for water so that my mom could cook.

At times it was hard for her even to get food. We would visit family members for lunch just so that we could eat. I remember days where all I ate was rice with ketchup on top of it. I didn't think too much about it at the time. I just thought it tasted pretty good, and I liked the nights we had rice and ketchup. You know, like *when is my mom going to make some rice and ketchup again?* I was young.

As I got older and started understanding the struggle, it got tough. Sometimes I was embarrassed that we could barely afford to live.

At the same time, that situation must have brought a lot of frustration for my mom. Toward the end of the seven years I spent in Colombia, our relationship wasn't so good. I would get in trouble for little things or no reason at all; I just happened to be the one there to take the blame.

During my time in Colombia, I would ride my bike to school and pay to park it or pay to ride the bus. But sometimes we didn't have the money for me to do either of those, so I would walk. I'm talking like a forty-five minute walk, depending on where we lived at any given time.

In Colombia, people will jump you and rob you just for a nice pair of shoes or a nice shirt. I was robbed twice. Once, I was coming out of school and two guys came up behind me; one of them grabbed my wrist while the other pulled out a knife. That time, they took my watch. A couple days later, someone tried to take a silver chain I had. I was walking out of school when the guy reached for it. He was my size, so I wasn't really scared until I saw all his friends. I took off running for home, so luckily I didn't get robbed that day.

But the second time I actually got robbed we had a school field trip to a water park on a Friday. Everyone had to get to the water park on their own. I left that morning on my bike with a friend. On the way over there, it was kind of ghetto, so we stayed on the road. We were going pretty fast, so we weren't worried about anything. When it was time to go back, I waited for a group of friends to leave so that I could leave with them and not be by myself. I figured if I left with a group of people it would be safer for me, but it didn't go as planned. I was messing with the gears on my bike riding around, so I started slowing down, and then two guys on another bike came by. One of them jumped off with a knife, grabbed my bike, and tried to stab me. A friend yelled out my name when he saw them approaching, so I turned around. When I saw the knife, I automatically jumped off the bike. These guys were pros.

As soon as I jumped off the bike, the guy jumped on it and rode it into his neighborhood. I had to make the two-hour walk back home.

There were a lot of situations like that over there. One of my friends got robbed at gunpoint. Someone pulled out a revolver and pointed it at his head just for a bike. It wasn't even a fancy, nice-looking bike.

I had to learn how to survive.

Zac

The need for resilience comes into play when you are taking a beating. When you are taking blow after blow, that is when your resilience will be tested. Sometimes we are required to test our resilience when things happen outside of our control, but other times we invite the test ourselves.

Inviting a test of resilience may be the reason somebody steps into a cage to fight. Or lines up on the start line for a difficult race. Or rides a bull. Or takes on any new challenge that provides the resistance and the beating they need to test their resilience.

On the other hand, some things happen that are out of our control that require us to test our resilience. The test is thrust upon you, and in my case that mandatory test was a cancer diagnosis. In these instances, our mindset can make or break our ability to be resilient. It's important to challenge your mindset. Do you look at this test as an opportunity for growth? Or do you look at it as something that happened to you and allow yourself to become a helpless victim?

I wasn't going to let my diagnosis slow me down.

Of course, there were times when the cancer treatment was hard, but it was important to me to keep up the habit of physical training regardless of the circumstances. As the treatments went on, I would be able to train for a while, and then I would not be able to for a while. The times after each surgery were my biggest gaps in training, but it was important for me to be in the gym as much as I could.

After I got my chemo port put in (a quick-channel device for chemotherapy that goes right into the veins underneath your skin, near the collarbone), I asked the doctors if I could still be on the mats training MMA. They told me the port was a pretty resilient piece of equipment, and that the mental and emotional benefits of training were worth the potential risks. Bethany was naturally worried every time I went to the gym. I mean, it was *during* chemo. My immune system was down, and there's always a higher chance for infection when people sweat and train. And at times I did have to pull back my training because my white blood cell count was nonexistent (meaning my immune system couldn't handle the stress or risk of infection that comes from being on the mats).

One of the most difficult parts of cancer treatment was the shots I had to get to boost my white blood cell count. The first couple of days after each shot were incredibly painful. The shots really do their job though, which is to help your body create new white cells from your bone marrow—an excruciating process. It feels like your body is one giant bruise from your internal organs to the outside of your skin. That part shut me down pretty good. I remember feeling terrible, and Bethany could do nothing to help. It was just too painful anytime someone touched me, and there was no relief. I knew if I could just stick it out for a few days, it would pass and I could get back to some sort of normalcy. Each time, as soon as I was able, I got back to work training.

Aside from my determination to stay as physically active as possible during my treatments, I used the extra time to work on a business plan. I wanted to utilize that time off and not let the cancer consume me—trying to use the opportunity instead of having a pity party. I had the time. If I had the energy to work on something, I felt bad if I wasn't trying to make progress somewhere. I felt like I was gifted an opportunity of time.

At the end of the day, you must decide that you are not going to let the circumstances dictate your results. You let your goals dictate your actions and reactions, and the circumstances can be overcome.

You keep going whenever and however you can. Whenever I got my shots, I knew the pain would eventually subside and be gone. And eventually the cancer was gone too.

Being Resilient Every Day

Choose to put one foot in front of the other and refuse to give up control of your life. What circumstances are testing your resilience right now? What is the first step you can take to move forward within those circumstances and regain control?

_____

_____

_____

_____

_____

_____

_____

_____

_____

_____

_____

_____

_____

_____

_____

_____

_____

_____

_____

_____

EXECUTING DECISIVENESS

Decisiveness is a characteristic of high-performing men and women. Almost any decision is better than no decision at all.
—**Brian Tracy**

What Does Executing Decisiveness Mean to Team KO?

Executing decisiveness means refusing to sit on the fence. It's making a plan and not doubting your decision once the choice is made. Instead, you follow through with that choice unless your way is proven wrong or counterintuitive.

Zac

I would be very surprised if any of us thought about backing out of *Spartan: Ultimate Team Challenge* for even a second. Although I have to say when I was peeing my pants at the starting line, I seriously considered not wanting to be there right then.

So yeah, fun fact: I peed myself at the starting line. I had no choice. I had to go. What I was not willing to do was risk not performing to my maximum potential during the race. I refused to blame losing on me having to pee. Not happening. There was a quarter-million dollars on the line. Would I rather have dry pants until the first obstacle or give myself a better chance of winning?

Decision made.

Okay, on a more serious note, our team exchanged a lot of back and forth on a particular obstacle for the show: the dreaded slip wall. We saw a few other teams doing it face-out, but we had practiced it face-in on a steeper wall and knew pretty confidently that it would work. But at the last minute there was a whole lot of questioning whether we should rethink our slip wall strategy. Was face-out better? Were we making the right call?

I remember Andres and I were particularly frustrated with the doubt. We had to put our foot down and say there was no way we were changing our plan so late in the game without ever having tried another method. We had done it face-in and knew that our method would work. No other team did it our way, so we had no reason to think that it wasn't a better way to do it. And we got practice time. It was no longer up for negotiation. That was the way we were going to do it.

Decision made. No more second-guessing.

Really, the slip wall was kind of a nightmare no matter what method we went with. I mean, getting over it seemed to be a nightmare for everybody else. We got over it just fine, but getting to that point was the nightmare. I don't think we faltered once on the actual wall, and we definitely didn't fall. We had a plan. Until that plan failed or proved wrong, we were going to stick to it. During training, we got a lot of practice at a totally sweet ninja gym that had a steeper wall than the one on the show. We just had to stick to our decision and what we had practiced and trust that it was the right one, no matter what everyone else was doing.

Executing Decisiveness Every Day

Trust your decisions. No decision means no progress. Right until proven wrong. Identify a decision that needs to be made in the immediate future. Select a deadline for that decision to be made, and carefully weigh the options. What are the pros and cons of each option?

_____

_____

_____

_____

_____

_____

_____

_____

_____

_____

_____

_____

_____

_____

_____

_____

_____

_____

_____

APPROACHING OBSTACLES WITH TENACITY

The most difficult thing is the decision to act,
the rest is merely tenacity.
—**Amelia Earhart**

What Does Approaching Obstacles with Tenacity Mean to Team KO?

When facing an obstacle, you have already overcome the hardest part: the decision to face that obstacle. To get past the obstacle, you must continue your approach without backing down—embrace an unrelenting resolve to keep putting one foot in front of the other by remembering why you chose to face that obstacle in the first place.

Jess

During the 2015 Spartan World Championship race, there was an especially cold-water swim when I thought I would actually fail.

How was I going to prepare to conquer that obstacle the next time?

For some people, the cold-water swim is easy. I hate that obstacle the most, both mentally and physically.

After that brutal cold-water swim, I tried doing cold-water training to prepare for the next one. I didn't do well with it. The swim was in sub-50-degree water, and it just took your breath away. But the obstacle was mandatory. You couldn't burpee out of it, and if you failed the swim you were disqualified. I made it through the swim. And even when I made it through that swim and emerged victorious on the other side, I had to tell the B*tch to shut up.

People look at our lives and think that everything is great, that everything goes smoothly and we accomplish our goals with no sweat off our backs. They have no idea how hard it is: the guts and tenacity it takes.

But no matter how hard it gets, I stand by my insistence that there are no limits to what people can accomplish. My "Jess No Limits" branding started because I was looking at that quote that says the sky is the limit, and it frustrated me. Because what is the sky really? I understand the whole concept, but to me naming the sky is still putting a limit on living life. We limit ourselves every single day, whether it's by fear, intimidation, anxiety, or random things that happen in life.

I limited myself for so long by providing myself with excuse after excuse. Anyone can find an excuse. Life happens. It doesn't matter who you are. We're all busy. Life happens. Tragedy happens. But when I changed my life, I promised myself that I wasn't going to let fear or emotions limit me anymore. Thus, no limits came into play.

A lot of people ask how I'm able to do all these Spartan races and travel everywhere.

Am I rich? No, I'm not.

Actually, I don't make a lot of money at all. Now, I could let that limit me, or I could find ways to make it happen despite the obstacles trying to block my path. We can do that with anything in life, but our minds put limits on us. I want to help people discover that they don't have limits, help them get past the mental blocks, and walk them through a situation. Sometimes people just need to hear what they *can* do instead of focusing on what they can't do, and that's the biggest tool I've been able to use to help others. I even do it to myself. Today. Tomorrow. Your brain builds walls around you, and you have to work to tear them down.

People look at me and think I'm a free bird with no fear, but really I'm a bird that fights fear and anxiety and panic and limits *all the time.* They think I have it together. Let me explain to you how I don't.

The tools I use to help others are the same tools I use myself every day. And I want to be able to embrace that. Even as a coach, I want to embrace the imperfections.

Limits only allow us to live within our comfort zone. When you start breaking down those walls, you move outside your comfort zone, and that's when real growth happens. It's not comfortable, but it needs to happen for any progress to occur.

When you approach an obstacle, you can't think about it. You just have to do it. Getting through that cold-water swim and not getting hypothermia require me to keep moving, to keep putting one foot in front of the other without stopping to think about it. I had to trust that my feet wouldn't fail, and if they did, that my hands wouldn't fail.

What's the worst that would have happened? I fall on my face?

In that case, I would have gotten right back up and kept going, kept getting over that obstacle to breathe on the other side. You just have to put one foot in front of the other, over and over again.

Andres

Facing obstacles requires tenacity. Whenever you have an obstacle in front of you and you're able to fight that obstacle, you get this feeling of invincibility. Pushing forward through something designed to stop your progress makes you feel unstoppable.

In reality, that's just not true. But it sure feels like it.

We're all human. There is a breaking point for everyone. There is a limit. If I take off running as fast as I can, eventually I'm going to slow down. I get tired. But if I possess the mental strength to exhaust 100 percent of my energy, I will die. That's my limit. We burn energy with everything we do. We get tired, slow down, gain more energy, and then keep going. Our bodies have a system that works. You run. You slow down, get your breath back, and keep going. You learn how to control your body to go the long distance. You might have an invincible mindset, but somewhere the body does have limits (although I'm sure Jess would disagree).

I'm not saying you're not capable of doing incredible things. All I'm saying is that we all reach a stopping point, but that doesn't mean our progress ends. That stopping point is just another obstacle, and we must condition ourselves to overcome it.

Nothing can stop you from accomplishing your goals. The body's limits are so far in the distance, I doubt anyone could ever find them. Even if you have a setback, you find your way back on course.

Here's how I see it: you have this obstacle, this mountain in front of you, and you don't know how you're going to cross it. You don't know how long it's going to take or how long the journey will be, but you're determined to cross it. The moment you get to the other side and realize the mountain is now behind you, you really do feel like you can do anything.

Give me a bigger mountain to climb.
Because I'm not going to stop.
Tenacity.

Zac

The most frustrating part of the *Ultimate Team Challenge* course came at the beginning of our first race.

One of the first obstacles was a wall much higher than any of us had been picturing, and it loomed there in front of us. It wasn't even the slip wall we had all been dreading.

We started with Andres and I getting the girls up. Next I helped Andres up, and it was then that I realized how hard it was going to be for me to get up.

Andres's arm was out waiting for me, so I went to grab it and my hand just slipped right off his arm. Not even close to holding on. We probably tried at least four times. We slipped, bonked forearms, high-fived—everything except what we needed to do.

And, let me tell you, everyone else on the other teams was over the wall after their first attempt, and at that point we were in last place.

I just remember thinking: *this is not happening right now.*

It was discouraging, but we had to keep trying. Stopping was not an option. We had to get through the obstacle.

Approaching Obstacles with Tenacity Every Day

Focus on the final goal instead of your weariness and limits. Maintain a strength of purpose. Identify a time when you wanted to give up in pursuit of a goal or overcoming an obstacle. How did you remain steadfast in your purpose?

_____

_____

_____

_____

_____

_____

_____

_____

_____

_____

_____

_____

_____

_____

_____

_____

_____

_____

_____

FOCUSING WITH INTENSITY

Always remember, your focus determines your reality.
—**George Lucas**

What Does Focusing with Intensity Mean to Team KO?

Focusing with intensity means zoning in on your goal, controlling your emotions, and doing whatever it takes to accomplish the goal. It means putting blinders on and not allowing yourself to be distracted or swayed from your plan.

Andres

After I graduated from boot camp, I headed to my first part of training for two months (before the actual SEAL training). The hardest part about that training for me was the water.

We did exercises where your hands and feet are tied, but you have to figure out how to swim anyway. And I'm not a fast swimmer. I can float; I can survive. I'm strong, just not fast.

The hardest part was being consistently last in a group of 150 guys. It was a struggle for me just to keep up with the pack when we were swimming. When you finish last every single time, it takes a toll on your confidence. There were a lot of times when it paid to be a winner because if you lost, you had to bear crawl around the pool, and it was a big Olympic-sized pool. The same thing went for training runs.

On the bright side, I got to a point where I was so good at bear crawling that it wasn't even a challenge anymore. That shows how often I came in last.

Besides coming in last, it was hard learning how to control myself during the underwater training. You're tied up and you have to swim without freaking out, keeping in mind that if you start to panic, you won't be able to think straight and will sink. So you have to calm yourself and acknowledge *yes, I am running out of breath,* and *yes, it does feel like I'm drowning.*

But you know that eventually you will be able to breathe again. You just have to hold on a little bit longer. It forces you to build that mental toughness, a lesson that took me a while to learn.

Pool training was on Wednesdays, so I was scared of Wednesdays. I knew what that day held, and I knew how it made me feel. I was afraid of freaking out. I didn't want to mess up, do something wrong. But you get better, get used to it.

After graduating that first training, I headed to San Diego where I continued my training. It was a lot of running, including running while carrying a boat over your head with seven other people, holding it down tight to keep it from bouncing. We were always wet from that point on.

When I wrestled in high school, I thought that would be the most intense training of my life. I couldn't imagine anything more intense than making it through that one season. I was wrong.

In San Diego, I felt the full force of intensity. I constantly acquired new cuts and scrapes on the back of my heels from my boots. They never healed because I was always wet, so I was limping all the time from the pain. And we had to run up to four miles through that excruciating pain. There was pain in my heels, on my lower back, neck, head, all from carrying the boat. My legs were sore. People wanted to quit. I watched people faint, and I watched people pretend to faint because they couldn't handle it.

Those were the times when adrenaline propelled me through and numbed anything and everything that hurt. I felt nothing. I had my mission, and I just went forward. It was intense like nothing I'd ever felt before.

That prolonged focus and intensity really breaks you down. Physically, it tears up your body, and it's mentally discouraging. It was hard to keep up. But it got to a point, especially with the boat runs, where quitting was no longer an option. I had come far enough that this was an obstacle I thought I could handle. Early in the training, I asked myself: *should I quit?* I didn't know if I would or not until I got to the point where I was too determined and had come too far not to finish the run for that day—no matter how much my body was telling me to stop.

As training went on, I found myself motivating and managing people a lot. Each crew that was carrying a boat had a boat crew leader, but I was afraid to take the title and be the one in charge. If you take charge and your crew messes up, it's your fault. It took me years to realize my reasons behind never taking the official leadership role, but I would move people around anyway. Certain spots were more challenging for some people than for others. So even refusing to take the official role, I was taking charge, swapping positions to give crewmembers a break. Helping others get through the training helped me as well.

Unfortunately, I did not make it through the training. I met with an obstacle I wasn't ready for at the time. However, all the training and lessons I gained from the experience did not go to waste, but helped me later in life.

Always wet. Always cold. But you have to keep moving forward.

Team KO

No matter how prepared we thought we were, there were points during *Ultimate Team Challenge* when we felt like the win would get away from us if we didn't get our act together.

In our first of the two races for the show, we failed miserably at one particular obstacle. There wasn't a lot of recovery time between our races. We had maybe two hours to rest up, and we spent most of that time strategizing. We hadn't gone out of our way to make friends before the competition. I mean, we were friendly to people we interacted with and were all about making friends afterwards, but we were there to compete. That meant being incredibly focused and intense.

Before any of the race days, NBC held a general rules meeting with all the teams who would compete on the show. They played a demonstration video of people going through the course and hitting all the obstacles, so we got a preview of how the obstacles were built and how they were conquered in the demonstration. There were certain rules and parameters for each obstacle, and we took detailed notes. This wasn't playtime. A quarter-million dollars was on the line, and that made most of the teams very focused.

With this high level of intensity, our team had to make a conscious effort to work together because that intensity is usually channeled during the individual struggles of fight camp. We had to remember that this was something for us to accomplish as a team. We had to keep each other in line and make sure everyone got to say what they needed to. We spent our evenings at the hotel strategizing, making sure we had the best plan for getting over each obstacle in the shortest amount of time. We cared about mere seconds, anything we could think of to save time or make an obstacle easier to complete. We even practiced how we were going to pick up a log in unison to make sure we did it the easiest way possible. We were doing everything we could to go into the race with our best game plan, and that involved keeping to ourselves most of the time and mentally rehearsing every step of the race.

We were there for a reason. We wanted to win. So when it came to that second round, we were ready to redo the obstacle we failed with a revised plan and actually got through it flawlessly. It was a matter of not letting the precious time we were losing get to our heads, keeping our cool, and focusing only on getting through the obstacle. We never once thought about the fact that there were cameras on us. We thought about wanting to win the race. The hardest part was when we knew we weren't in the lead. Knowing that someone else is beating you makes it easy to let doubt get in your head and disrupt that focus and intensity. But you can't take yourself out of the game like that. You have to keep focus even when it feels like you're not accomplishing what you wanted to accomplish.

In general, our game plan served us very well. We lost to the team that won the whole competition. Even the teams whose times we beat had faster times than the majority of competitors. We did really, really well, which made not winning frustrating. But the planning paid off. And so did our focus.

So yeah, the money would have been amazing, but it was still the pride of winning and being the best team that we really missed out on.

Zac

The biggest tool for remaining focused is learning to say no.

There will always be a million things pulling you in as many different directions. The key is not letting them distract you—by saying no. It's not always easy, but there's not much more to it than that.

The potential results from staying focused are unlimited. For me, it has provided the ability to start a business in an industry where I was a complete unknown and become one of the top producers in that space. That has required intense focus and a commitment to *staying* focused every single day regardless of the many distractions that pop up.

I evaluate each new thing that crosses my path, and I say no to most of them. It's as simple as that.

Focusing with Intensity Every Day

Staying focused is crucial to accomplishing any goal. Knowing how to keep yourself on track is highly valuable. What are some tactics that work for you when you're trying to focus?

_____

_____

_____

_____

_____

_____

_____

_____

_____

_____

_____

_____

_____

_____

_____

_____

_____

_____

_____

_____

_____

_____

PRIORITIZING FITNESS AND SELF-CARE

Never underestimate the investment you make in yourself.
—Unknown

What Does Prioritizing Fitness and Self-Care Mean to Team KO?

Prioritizing fitness and self-care means taking care of yourself: body, mind, and heart. It's educating yourself on all aspects of your individual wellness and being okay with where you are in your journey. Your self-care is your base for greatness.

Andres

As I mentioned earlier, I made my own dumbbell when I was fourteen with cement blocks in Colombia. Then when I started high school in the States, I discovered the gym in the basement—and I loved it.

Every day after school, I would go straight to the gym and spend an hour or two there. For the first couple of months, I still was doing only bicep curls, although with actual dumbbells this time. That was all I knew. I wouldn't do any cardio whatsoever. I picked things up and put them down until one day I noticed people doing other workouts and other machines. During gym class, we would spend time in the weight room, and all the other guys made a big deal about the bench press and how much they could put up. Everyone would gather around the bench press, and it made me curious. I wanted to try and see what I could do.

So I started doing the bench press, and I still had no idea what it worked out. I didn't know what I was doing. I was grabbing something heavy and pushing it because it fascinated me, but I enjoyed it enough that eventually I wanted to learn about what I was doing.

Throughout high school, I learned how to use one machine at a time. When I saw someone doing a new machine, I would go home and research, reading any articles I could find. Slowly, I learned that I needed to work different muscles in different ways. I developed routines focused on bodybuilding, but never really got big, just very cut up. I maintained a meathead mentality until I tried out for wrestling my junior year.

At that point, I thought because I could bench press and squat and was bigger than someone else, I could beat them. But I remember how the smallest guy on the wrestling team threw me around that first day, and I couldn't figure out what was going on.

That's when I realized there must be more to overall fitness than I previously understood. I didn't have cardio as a part of my routine, so I started implementing that into my workouts. Then I added technique, and so on, until I educated myself and learned how many different parts of fitness there really are.

And I'm still learning.

Jess

When I decided to take steps toward getting out of my dark place, I joined a writers' group. The group was not meant to be a form of rehab and had no association with AA. Everyone in the group had something to work through, and there was an element of accountability with our writing mentor. The writing was meant to be a tool for life.

When I first called my writing mentor, she didn't even want to hear my story. All she wanted to know was what I was dealing with: Drugs? Pills? What was my deal? She wanted me to lay it out plain and simple.

Then all she said was: "Cut it off."

My breath caught in my throat. She was serious. I never once told her that I would never drink again. Cutting off drinking entirely was not the original game plan.

"I want you to call me before noon every day. Write three pages to God. If you don't believe in God, write three pages to your higher power or whatever it is that you believe in. Call me when your pages are done. I only have two rules. One, the morning phone call is mandatory. Two, if you want to go back out and drink, that's fine. Just don't ever call me again and don't waste my time."

And that was that.

So I agreed and started working through my emotions, and all these buried feelings bubbled out when I wrote.

There's magic in the writing.

You sit, staring at the blank page, and write: Dear God. The pen hovers over the paper as you wonder: *what can I write for three pages?*

Let me tell you, as soon as you let your pen form the first sentence, any sentence, three pages flies by. It may start with just telling God what you have going on that day, and somehow it spins into spilling guilty feelings for things you did or things you don't remember because you were blacked out drunk. I had a lot of things to deal with, and those pages were always filled.

As I was going through the process of the writers' group, guilt over not prioritizing self-care was a big thing that came up.

One day I wrote a letter—the same letter I wrote every day, just different words—and in that letter I wrote about how I had failed to take care of my body for so many years. I wanted to get healthy overall: mind, body, and heart. The question was: *what am I going to do to take care of my body now?* It all came in baby steps. There was no instant healing or miraculous moment where I suddenly felt healthy.

As I started the journey, I realized that it's not about being physically fit as much as it's about being mentally fit. The physical part is just a bonus, as far as body and looks, but it really starts on the inside. Gaining weight and becoming so careless about my self-care sparked a desire to take better care of myself physically, but the physical and mental parts go hand-in-hand.

I tried getting physically fit before I made any mental shift. I would go to group fitness classes, jumping around to any class that I could. Then I did some small challenges—mud runs, stair climbs, 5Ks, etc. I didn't start with a Spartan race. And it's funny because I felt like I barely made it through the first 5K I tried. I remember tripping in cornfields and being miserable in cold-water obstacles when I tried racing in November. But when I mentally and physically completed what seems like a tiny race now, I felt like I had accomplished something for the first time in a long time.

What could I do next?

I went from small challenge to small challenge after that: cross fit, tire flipping, just a little bit of everything, but small and different every time. I would pick something quarterly to work toward, and that's how I would stay in the gym. But I still had one foot in each world.

I was still mentally unhealthy, getting trashed on a regular basis while trying to maintain good fitness, and it was depressing because it made me disappointed in who I was.

I say it starts with mental self-care, but your physical self-care can oftentimes reflect your mental self-care, or even spark mental self-care. The two are always intertwined. I have to consciously make myself take care of my mind and heart—embracing spirituality, educating myself, growing, and learning. The mental self-care is different for everybody, and you have to find what works for you. Even on days when I have so much going on and I'm super stressed, I make sure to address all parts of self-care.

When I really started pursuing self-care—mind, body, and heart— the most important thing I did physically was just start running. Everyone wants to know when I ran, where I ran, how far I ran, how I ran, and I just tell them to start. Do the 3/3: three miles, three times a week. Start there. Start small. Get consistent with it. When you get consistent with it, then we'll talk (that's the coach in me coming out).

But seriously, once you get consistent, then you can move on to step two. Baby steps are okay.

People don't want to take the time to build a base. They're impatient and want to jump to the top. I understand not wanting to build a base. It takes months to build. I feel like I'm still building my base two years later. You can't build a base and stop. It's frustrating. It's boring. It's tedious. Truthfully, it's kind of terrible. But that's sacrifice: going out there and doing it. The key for me was changing my perspective. When I do go through training slumps, I listen to MMA motivational training videos. They drive me to keep going. People use all kinds of unique motivations to remind them why they go out and push through the slumps and the base building.

Eventually that 3/3 becomes 3/4 and you just continue to build from there. After my running increased, I quickly learned how important strength is. When I made the transition from group fitness to having enough motivation to train on my own, I learned that finding a coach is so helpful. It holds you accountable and gives you someone who is there for you both mentally and physically. It's the way to go. Otherwise, you're left to your own discretion. I don't care who you are, being on your own doesn't always work.

My mentality going into training was that if I worked hard, I would be able to fly. But I've found that is not always true. There's a science behind it, and learning that came with educating myself.

But it all starts with getting up, just doing it, and prioritizing your self-care every day.

Prioritizing Fitness and Self-Care Every Day

Learning to prioritize self-care takes time and practice. Start with the basics and educate yourself one step at a time, keeping in mind that self-care is not just physical. What will be your first step toward better self-care? mentally? physically? emotionally?

_____

_____

_____

_____

_____

_____

_____

_____

_____

_____

_____

_____

_____

_____

_____

_____

_____

_____

_____

_____

LEARNING FROM FAILURE

We define ourselves far too often by our past failures.
That's not you. You are this person right now. You're
the person who has learned from those failures. Build
confidence and momentum with each good decision
you make here on out, and choose to be inspired.
—Joe Rogan

What Does Learning from Failure Mean to Team KO?

Learning from failure means accepting that loss is a part of life and letting those losses fuel your desire to come back and win. It also means paying attention to the failures of others and not repeating those mistakes.

Bethany

Failure can be a hotbed for self-deprecation. It can cause you to scrutinize every mistake you made that resulted in failure and beat yourself up with things like negative self-talk, doubt, and regret. Failure can also be a powerful catalyst for growth, self-acceptance, and learning.

In 2013, I competed on the TV show *The Ultimate Fighter*. It was unlike anything I was used to. This was the first season for women to compete on the show, and the national attention surrounding it meant the stakes were high for everyone involved. I went in with confidence in my technique; however, going up one weight class for the show put me at a physical disadvantage. I didn't walk away with the win that day.

I put a lot on the line personally for this fight. Given how high-profile the event was and what it meant for women in the sport, losing sent additional shockwaves of failure through my system that I felt more acutely than the physical punches thrown at me in the cage. It was a dark moment for me.

When I returned home, I went for a long walk on a trail near my house. The trail is situated along the James River, boasting one of the best sunset views in the city, creating space for quiet contemplation and self-reflection. For me, self-reflection leads to a more complete perspective and therefore a better understanding of myself. And after my loss at *Ultimate Fighter*, I needed some perspective.

As I watched the sun sink below the horizon I realized it would not have been beautiful were it all light. The shadow spots of darkness created the sky's depth, dimension, character, and ultimately beauty. And I acknowledged that failure has the power to enrich my own character if I choose to learn from my mistakes and integrate those lessons into the landscape of my life.

While it's hard to keep this in mind in the moment, realize that whoever you are, wherever you are, and whatever you're doing, YOU are in control of your daily decisions, habits, thoughts, and ultimately your path in life. It is up to you to decide how you will incorporate things like failure into the landscape of your life. By owning the darkness, you choose to expand your depth and strengthen your character.

I started my walk feeling overwhelmed by the failure of my recent loss. But I returned home feeling fully at peace. The loss was still there, but I could honestly say I was glad I showed up to compete and was thankful for the lessons that failure brought me.

I refused to allow my failure to define my worth as a person. Instead I chose to continue on my path of becoming a better fighter and a better human being.

I can't wait to fight again.

Zac

We talk about all these failures in our lives, all these times where we've fallen short and somehow had to stand back up. Most of those times in my life involved failed business plans. And, yes, maybe one certain business plan didn't amount to anything, so looking back I guess it is a failure. That's how I technically classify it. But the time you put into failures certainly isn't wasted time. All the lessons I learned about what not to do apply to other business ventures that I pursue. It may have seemed like time wasted for that particular project, but it yielded lessons for my future.

What I have learned is that you have to know when your shoes are too big. The project I was going for involved some pretty big shoes to fill. The scope of the project was beyond my capabilities then and might still be beyond my capabilities now. Abandoning that project feels like failure, but in reality it's more of a pause before I can come back. It's not going away. I still think about it regularly. It's a great idea about building a Tiny House community that reframes house ownership and makes it less daunting for people who don't want to pay a mortgage for fifteen to thirty years.

Don't ever get me started talking about Tiny House community because I will not stop talking, and it will happen someday. But right now I'm working full-time with Leaderboard and learning how to be patient and bide my time, focusing on the things I want to and *can* do now. When the time is right for Tiny House community and other ideas that may have not panned out in the past, I'll have the chance to give them my all.

Loss always motivates me to keep fighting. Losing is a taste you can't rinse out of your mouth until you win again. It's sour and salty and gross, and you don't want it there, but the only way to get rid of it is to come back and win.

Every title fight I had until my most recent one, I lost. That's incredibly frustrating because those are the fights where it's important to win. I take a lot of pride in excelling during high-pressure situations. Sure, any time you go into a fight, it's a high-pressure situation, but when you put a regular fight next to a title fight, the stakes shoot way up. That's your new high-pressure gauge. So losing every time it counted sucked. But, again, I didn't want to stop fighting on a loss. I wanted to prove that I deserved another opportunity, instead of wasting the lost fight or not learning what I could from it. It's the same with any other kind of competition.

You lose, and you want to come back and win.

Learning from Failure Every Day

Let your failures be your motivation, and learn from those shortcomings. Reflect on the most recent time that you came up short. What can you take away from that experience that will help you in your next attempt?

_____

_____

_____

_____

_____

_____

_____

_____

_____

_____

_____

_____

_____

_____

_____

_____

_____

_____

_____

_____

_____

_____

_____

DEFINING SUCCESS

Next to excellence is the appreciation of it.
—**William Makepeace Thackeray**

What Does Defining Success Mean to Team KO?

Success looks different to each person. Defining success means identifying what success looks like to you and recognizing it when you get there. For some, that might mean simply showing up to race, for others it might be landing on the podium, and for still others it may very well be going for the win. Whatever you define as success, the important part is stopping to appreciate your effort and letting it sink in before immediately raising the bar.

Bethany

I was undefeated as a professional fighter when Zac got sick. My MMA record was 4-0. When we got the news about his cancer, I had a fight lined up and had already signed the contract. It was the only fight I've ever backed out of.

Zac's first round of chemo was supposed to start on a Monday, and I was scheduled to leave for my fight the very next day. I knew I would never be able to focus on the job at hand if I went. I didn't feel confident that I was ready to go into this fight and give it my all while Zac was sick in a hospital bed, so I backed out. After that, I still trained when I could, but getting him through his treatments and surgeries was on the front burner for that whole two-year season of our lives. I don't regret that whatsoever.

When Zac finally got the "all clear," I felt ready to fight again. I signed a contract to fight for Invicta Fighting Championships, the largest women's MMA promotion in the world. I trained hard, but I didn't anticipate just how much two years off from training and fighting would slow me down. I was not as prepared as I should have been and faced a fighter who had made massive improvements to her fight game. She was on the rise while I was just getting back into the game, and she was the wrong person for me to fight that night. Ring rust mixed with a high-level opponent was not a good combination.

While some may see that loss as failure, in my mind it involved a lot of success since that fight got me back in the game and marked the end of our two-year battle with Zac's cancer.

Success stories are boring if they don't include struggle. You cannot judge your personal success based on anyone else's expectations, good or bad.

You define your own success.

Andres

During the first two years of high school, my fitness routine included lifting only. Somehow I remained skinny but was pretty cut up. Classmates saw that I was strong and asked me to join the wrestling team, but I didn't think the sport was for me. I wanted to try out for the football team instead, even though I had never played football.

In Colombia, I only saw basketball and soccer. Everyone played soccer. Even people who didn't play soccer played soccer. I was never much good at those sports, but I wanted to give a new sport a try, and I liked the popular associations with football.

Like I said, I had the strength, so I thought I would be great at football. I imagined myself as a beast during tryouts, making it through with flying colors. I didn't even know what a quarterback was. I didn't know any positions. I ran, caught the ball, and that was it—a primitive understanding. And I got pushed around because I didn't have a lot of friends. I admit that I sucked at football, but the other guys pushed me around unnecessarily.

I stayed and went through all the tryouts, but when I made it to the end I stopped going. I didn't fit in.

Once the school year got underway, it felt awful whenever the football team would come back from a win celebrating. Everyone was ecstatic, and I felt left out. I could have been a part of their celebration. Even though I sucked, I could have pushed myself through a season and at least know that I tried, and maybe I would have improved. That terrible feeling of being a quitter motivated me to eventually join wrestling. As far as I knew before joining, weight class determined wrestling match opponents, and it was one-on-one during competition. In a way, it was like I had an opportunity to face myself because I would be matched up with a guy my size. It wasn't a team sport. Once you step on that mat, it's one-on-one. I saw it as a test—a way to prove myself and display how tough I could be. It wasn't until a year after quitting football, my junior year, that I finally got the chance to try out.

My junior year was my only season on the wrestling team. I found the sport demanding both mentally and physically. I stopped working out on my own, going from lifting before practice and doing my pushups and sit-ups at night, to completely dropping both of those routines. By the time I got home from wrestling practice, I was exhausted. I'd go home, take a shower, and just lie on the couch. That kind of exhaustion was something new to me.

I finished with a record of eight wins and sixteen losses in the 145-150 weight class, which was pretty good for my first year of wrestling. Especially considering that a lot of the schools we went up against were good schools with guys who had been wrestling for years.

Despite my relatively good record, the matches still frustrated me because it felt like every time I would win one battle, I lost two. The mental adjustment of accepting the loss potential was far more challenging than the physical adjustments. Every day at practice, I thought about quitting. I thought I wasn't good enough or that maybe wrestling just wasn't for me. I was sore. I was tired. I felt muscles I didn't even know I had. But I kept giving it another try.

The first time I won was a home match. I snapped my opponent to the ground, flipped him over, and pinned him. I had him beat within a minute, and it was one of the most exciting moments of my life. The crowd was screaming and celebrating because I had just won. That boosted my confidence levels, and for the first time I thought I could do this. I could be successful at wrestling.

But, again, it was win one, lose two, and those losses were hard to overcome.

I saw the losses as a reflection of insufficient skill. I thought I lost because I sucked. I felt like there was nothing I could do. Every day at practice, there was a mental struggle with the voice in my head telling me I wasn't ready for this, telling me to quit. It was tempting, but then I would remember when I tried out for football and how wimpy I felt after quitting. Physically, maybe I never would have been good enough, but mentally I should have bucked up. That was something I could have controlled. The memory of how quitting felt pushed me through the whole wrestling season and kept me motivated through all the losses and all the internal battles. The feelings associated with quitting never change, no matter the circumstances or how old you are.

In the end, I regretted not joining the team earlier because I really loved it. I loved the competition. It made me feel strong. Whenever you win and get your hand raised, you just bask in the glory. You look at everyone cheering and see all your hard work reflected in the win. You went out there and used every technique you knew, and it paid off.

On the other hand, losses always remained tough. I didn't deal with them well, but the important part is to keep pushing through and moving forward no matter what.

Until you win.

Jess

The way I see it, you don't fail unless you quit.

During the 2015 Spartan World Championship, a brutal fifteen-mile OCR in the mountains, my body was breaking down. My foot was in intense pain, but honestly I think a lot of it was in my head.

At the time, I thought it might have been broken, but I got to the finish line and my foot wasn't even that bad. My shoulder sure felt out of place though, and my thumb was bleeding, but all I could do was hold it because you were out of the race as soon as medical touched you. Your body can always do so much more, but it's your mind that plays tricks on you. It was crazy getting to the finish line and discovering that my crushed bones and gaping gashes were mere scrapes and bruises.

I felt unbreakable afterwards.

As I was doing the Ultra Beast later that year, I held onto that unbreakable feeling.

Completing two laps of a Spartan beast race back to back in New Jersey terrain, we gained over eleven thousand feet in elevation and ran more than thirty miles total. I thought I would break down after mile twenty. The race took us eleven hours, which sounds about right for thirty miles, but it would have taken Andres and I less time if we hadn't stayed at the midway point for so long.

We rested at the midway point for about an hour, changing our shoes and trying to eat, wondering *how are we going to do this again?* My stomach was a wreck during the first lap, mostly from nerves and trying to carb load with junk food that my body just isn't used to processing. And I didn't know if the pain was going to stop. I mean, after five and a half hours, my stomach was still in knots. There was a gremlin in my stomach, and I smashed my toe and didn't know how the second lap was going to go, but then I went into game mode after leaving the midway point.

Thankfully, my stomach was feeling better by then, but I had smashed my knee pretty badly, and once I started climbing again it was like my body didn't want to go. I just kept going anyway.

I have this Spartan bracelet, and on the bottom side it says "Unbreakable." That's what I kept saying in my head: *unbreakable, unbreakable, unbreakable.*

Even if I had actually broken something, I'm pretty sure I would have crawled to finish. I was in game mode. My body went numb, and somewhere along the way I realized that I was flying—and ended up placing sixteenth. Because I kept going.

Success.

Team KO

You know what's crazy? We didn't win our second race on *Ultimate Team Challenge*, but we celebrated as if we had won when we finished. Part of it was that we were all just glad to be done.

What are the things we're supposed to say about losing?

It's still a success . . .

It was a learning experience . . .

We were so successful in finishing . . .

We did our best . . .

Don't be a sore loser.

Blah blah blah.

But all jokes aside, we *are* going to see the benefits of the experience, despite it still feeling like a failure. People were excited to watch the show, and the *experience* was a success. We got selected for the show in the first place. We competed. We did great. We almost won!

Talking about success, we're trying to embrace all the opportunity that the show provided. For one, it brought us together. We became more like family than friends. We were training with each other all the time, and just training together pushed us ten times closer.

It was also an educational experience. We went into *Ultimate Team Challenge* saying that whether we won or lost, we weren't going to waste the opportunity. Even if we didn't win, we wanted to do something with the experience (like this book).

That being said, we did fully expect to win. But one of the things we've all learned is that, win or lose, you have to learn something to make each experience worthwhile.

Your fans almost love you a little bit more when you lose because it shows that you're human too. You get a chance to see who's in your corner.

Not only that, but you really get to know yourself. If you're successful all the time at everything you do, how do you know what you can withstand? There's certainly nothing wrong with winning, but when you fall to the bottom, how will you stand back up? That's when you find out how strong you are, how much pressure, disappointment, and humility you can stomach without breaking. It might feel lonely. Even if you have the support of other people, you came up short when they helped you get ready and believed in you, and that's hard.

We had an advantage over some of the other teams on the show because, in our own ways, we've each lost in life. We've lost fights or in our personal lives or have quit when we knew we should have persevered. We've all had to face that let-down and disappointment before, so we all were able to reframe it as less of a loss. We're still annoyed by the loss. We all wanted to win. Who doesn't? But you should come back stronger from a loss and do everything possible to set yourself up for the next opportunity.

That's success.

Defining Success Every Day

Define success for yourself. Identify one area of your life where you strive to achieve success. What would you consider to be success in that area? When you reach success in that area, how will you celebrate? How long will you take to pause and let it sink in before raising the bar?

_____

_____

_____

_____

_____

_____

_____

_____

_____

_____

_____

_____

_____

_____

_____

_____

_____

_____

_____

_____

_____

UNDERSTANDING SACRIFICE

If you don't sacrifice for what you want,
what you want will be the sacrifice.
—Unknown

What Does Understanding Sacrifice Mean to Team KO?

There will be things in your life that you have to sacrifice to achieve your goals. Understanding and choosing to make those sacrifices will lay the groundwork for success and later opportunities.

Team KO

A lot of the sacrifices our team made for the show were made long before the show was even in the picture. We like to think of it as blind sacrifice: training and being prepared for opportunities that might arise and outcomes you can't see yet. It's putting yourself out there and working hard without knowing exactly what the reward will be.

There's no denying that it's easier to make sacrifices if you know exactly what's in front of you, but all of us had already made sacrifices in our individual lives with training, so when the opportunity to be on *Ultimate Team Challenge* came around, we were ready. We didn't know what the outcome would be, but we decided to capitalize on it because the sacrifices had already been made. We were already doing every day what preparing for the show required of us: working hard to be the best people we could be and training athletically.

When the opportunity to be on the show came, already being prepared physically and mentally allowed us to spend Labor Day weekend together filming the videos. Lo and behold, we were the first team to be selected. Not because we found out, started training, and decided to be a Spartan team three weeks before filming. The sacrifices that helped our chances of success were made by Jess years ago training for Spartan races, or by Zac and Bethany training for MMA fights, or by Andres constantly expanding his athletic horizons. All of us coming together was just the culmination of that training and sacrifice. We made those sacrifices before even becoming a team and trained individually without the lofty intention of the show in front of us.

Laying the groundwork for years was the patient and grinding preparation for this unknown opportunity. Standing ready year-round, no matter what else we have going on, is something we all take pride in. It's a mental grind. But it pays off.

Jess

The sacrifice it takes to prioritize self-care is everything sometimes. It's choosing to complete your second training session of the day while all your friends are asking you to go out to dinner with them, or waking up at 5 a.m. for quiet time, or having to bring work and training on family vacations. Sometimes I even sacrifice time with my family. I advocate a healthy balance, but that doesn't mean you never have to sacrifice.

And it can be financial sacrifice too. People think I make a lot of money to be able to compete and travel all over the US as often as I do, but the only way I'm able to do this is by being financially thrifty. I don't go out to eat all the time. I stopped spending money at 7-Eleven. There were a lot of financial adjustments for me, even housing-wise. I can't live somewhere with expensive rent if I'm going to be traveling all the time.

There have been days when I've worked all day and trained all evening, and I get home and just want the down-time to relax, but I have to walk my dog and give him the little bit of attention I have left before heading to bed to do it all over again.

Sacrifice is huge. It's not for everyone, and I don't think people really understand it or always act on it if they do. That sacrifice looks different for everyone. There have been times when I've felt incredibly lonely because everyone else was out doing activities together and having fun while I was in the gym training. Oftentimes people will look to fill that void with unhealthy vices, but that's when you have to stay focused. Know that the sacrifice for your self-care will pay off.

Balancing it all has been my biggest challenge, and I'm not always successful. Having people in your life who support you is essential. Most people won't understand. I have friends who see me on Facebook and want to grab dinner, and when I have to get my training done instead, who is really going to understand that? The response is usually to give me a hard time, which is flattering, but at the same time you want the people closest to you to understand that what you're doing is hard work. Their support is a huge factor in keeping it all from driving you to a breaking point.

If I didn't have anyone supporting me, it would be much more difficult. But if there are times when no one supports you, what do you do then?

That's when you have to sacrifice.

Like I said, I deal with lonely feelings at times, like I'm in this all by myself. But I know that I'm not. Those feelings and living in the pain are all a part of the sacrifice to be where I am and push myself toward where I want to be. I can't give up. I can't wallow in self-pity because I remember why I'm there, why I do what I do. It's hard to pinpoint it all, but the sacrifice is huge.

You can't dwell in self-pity or contemplate your sacrifice or live in the past. You can't focus on imperfections in your attempt to find a healthy balance, but must continuously move forward. Embrace the pain and the process that are part of sacrificing, and recognize that sacrifice is a part of life. You can't have everything all the time. Focusing on the pain that comes along with sacrifice does no good. Remember that success won't happen without sacrifice.

Acknowledge the sacrifices you make for your success, embrace the process, and strive for a balance. And, most importantly, remember that you are only human.

Bethany

All goals require sacrifice to their own degree. Sacrifice, like any quality or characteristic, can be either healthy or unhealthy depending on the extreme to which you take it.

Healthy sacrifice is sacrificing the right short-term desires for the sake of long-term goals, and being willing to give up what you want in the moment if it doesn't align with your big picture. Unhealthy sacrifice is when the sacrifice becomes all-consuming and you lose sight of the big picture of where a particular goal or sacrifice for the goal fits in relation to your whole life.

The decision of what things are worth sacrificing for the big picture will be different for everyone. I've been lucky in that Zac and I have similar goals and dreams. He doesn't make me feel like I'm choosing between him and my goals. That's ultimately what it comes down to: the people in your life who really love and care about you will stay supportive of you if you're going after something, even if that means you can't spend the time with them that you want to. That's the kind of support I want to give to Zac and others in my life who are working toward their own goals.

The fear of missing out hinders a lot of people from doing the hard thing and saying no when they need to. But keep in mind when faced with a detour that when you say yes to the wrong things, you are saying no to the right thing. Question each opportunity that comes your way: *how will this impact my goal?* And then weigh the answer—it's up to you to evaluate each opportunity that presents itself. *Will this inhibit my goal? Is this worthy of my time? Will I regret making this decision if it is the one thing that hinders me from reaching my goal?*

The results of your sacrifice may not show themselves overnight. This is the phase in which you must be most diligent. We live in a time of instant gratification, and it can be frustrating and sometimes discouraging if you don't see the results right away. This is where the truly determined stand out from the rest of the crowd, the moment that successful people make the decision to keep their noses to the grindstone, not allowing themselves to be deterred.

The sacrifices become easier to make as they become habitual. Once new habits are formed, they can even become enjoyable. Instead of looking at it like *I have to give this up* or *I'm missing out on this,* look at it like *I am one step closer to my goal.*

Understanding Sacrifice Every Day

While sacrifice is unavoidable, it should not be permanent or long-term. Balance keeps you from reaching a breaking point. Identify some things you know you will have to sacrifice to achieve a specific goal. Does the end goal outweigh the sacrifice? How will you keep the sacrifice within healthy limits?

_____

_____

_____

_____

_____

_____

_____

_____

_____

_____

_____

_____

_____

_____

_____

_____

_____

_____

_____

_____

Conclusion

THE SLIP WALL

There it was, looming through the trees as they rounded the corner of the course. This was the obstacle they'd trained for, prepared for. Even though most of the other teams decided to face out, pushing their backs against the slip wall, Team KO stuck with their plan.

Andres plopped straight against the wall, face smeared in the mud, blind to what everyone else was doing, but trusting them to get it done. Zac clambered onto his shoulders and stood in the same manner, facing inward, relying on his teammates to continue the process. Bethany climbed them like they were a human rope, to stand on Zac's shoulders, followed by Katie, before Jess climbed all four to be the first one to the top.

The empty pages mock me. I didn't start with the intention of never picking up a drink again. Those were my writing mentor's words, not mine. I grip my pen tightly, hovered over the creamy clean slate of a blank page. My throat tightens, trying to suffocate all the emotions buried for so long that want to leap onto the page. The easy thing to do would be to never call my writing mentor again. I could put this pen down and shovel the dirt right back over all the guilt, the fear, the shame, and leave the world with only the image of my life as a clean white sheet of paper. But then I remember death. And I slowly lower my hand to the paper and mar it with the black ink: Dear God. The midnight words flow swiftly once the first sentence is written. The creamy slate is soon coated with black markings, swimming across the page in an endless stream, as if putting the pen to paper wrecked the dam on my heart. The first tear falls. Where it lands, the ink ripples out like my emotions seem to be doing without my permission. The creamy slate isn't real; it's gone. It's now gray and black and messy. And mine. You know, people saw me as the strong person—the one who never let anything get to her, never let anything disrupt that white sheet of paper. But I wasn't. I am now. I wasn't then.

Jess propelled herself over her four teammates, hoisting herself onto the top of the wall before turning around to help Katie do the same. Once Katie and Jess were securely on top of the wall, they each grabbed one of Bethany's arms. Zac wrapped his arms around Bethany's feet as Jess and Katie slid her body farther up the wall. Bethany's arms felt like they just might be ripped out of their sockets before this was over, with Zac and Andres's weight fully held up by her arms. She couldn't do anything except dangle like the human rope she was, trusting Jess not to drop her. Jess stared right at Bethany, yelling "I got you" over and over.

I can't see the crowd surrounding the ring. All I see is the girl in front of me. My mind is steel. There's a wall blocking out the doubt, the fear, any emotion that might distract from the goal in front of me: to beat this girl. All my concentration goes toward maintaining the mental stronghold and controlling my breathing. One, two, three, in. One, two, three, out—trying to slow down my heart, which is pulsing so hard that it feels like with each beat it increases in size, slowly blocking the air trying to get into my lungs, building another wall in my windpipe. One, two, three, in. One, two, three, out. In this ring, no one else matters. I raise my hands in front of my face: my only defense against the blows to come. There are no teammates waiting to jump in and throw punches on my behalf. It's me versus her. I stand alone in the ring.

Bethany held fast.

"I got you," Zac heard ringing out in Jess's commanding voice, as all he could see in front of him was the muddy wall. Andres continued to use Zac as a human rope as he climbed over his body and then Bethany's, held in place only by Jess and Katie's strength. One teammate at a time, Andres scaled the slip wall.

I feel the insistent request for relief coming from my opponent. I feel each muscle fiber relax after the prolonged tension I've held them to. My hand is raised in the air. I thought I'd be depending on the referee to keep it in the air after the intensity and energy required by the fight, but I feel strong. I could hold my arm up all day long. For the first time, I see the crowd. It's a blur of faces, all cheering for me. I see the hard work put in, the days of training, of forcing myself to go to the gym after a long day of work or no sleep. I see the days I drove home barely able to keep my hands on the wheel. But doing it all over again the next day anyway. The pride swells up in my throat as I finally acknowledge everything I've been feeling for weeks, letting the solid wall around my emotions crumble, feeling on top of the world.

Zac was less than a second away from slipping back down to the bottom as he felt Andres climbing over him. He was losing his grip on Bethany's shoes after he tried to say something to his teammates and his grip shifted. He could feel her shoe slowly slipping out of the crook of his arm.

I can't train. My entire body aches like it's all part of one giant bruise. Everything from my internal organs to the tips of my fingers feels like it's been pummeled. Bethany lightly rubs my back to try and comfort me, and it's like she's applying an entire ton of pressure directly to my wound—except my wound is my whole body. I can barely move, and the easiest thing for me to do would be to lie as still as a corpse and wait for the pain to pass. A flicker of rebellion flashes across my conscious as I wince and consider that option. I never wanted to let the cancer consume me; my body was broken but I had the mental energy, the fight, to do something with that time. I slowly pulled out my iPad and began formulating a business plan. Between the surgeries and the bruising shots, I was incapacitated long enough to write one from start to finish. Every time I gave in, feeling the pain of this consuming illness, it was like a voice in my head reminded me that progress is always possible. I've been gifted an opportunity of time. I can't train. I can't work. What can I do? Just hold on.

As Bethany's shoe slowly made its escape, Zac scrambled to hold on until the last second as Andres's weight pushed off his shoulder.

Don't even tell them that you're slipping right now. Almost there. No time for delay.

It was get over the wall now or fall.

Team KO might get portrayed as "superheroes," but none of them are any different from anyone else, and every accomplishment comes with its own struggle and its own sacrifices.

What's your slip wall?

ACKNOWLEDGMENTS

Team KO would like to thank and acknowledge the following people for your contributions to our lives and careers that led us to this point.

Our families: you are who shaped us into the people we are today. Especially our moms, Scottie Marshall, LeeAnn Lowman, Paula Burton, and Julieta Encinales.

Our martial arts and OCR coaches and teammates: you helped shape us into the athletes and competitors we are. You've taken us to our breaking point and taught us so much.

Morgan James Publishing: thank you for publishing our book and all the behind-the-scenes work you do in helping us take stories from a manuscript to a book. We would especially like to thank David Hancock, Jim Howard, Margo Toulouse, and Nickcole Watkins.

Thank you to Amber Johnson for your art contribution!

Aubrey Kosa: from the bottom of our hearts we thank you for the countless hours you invested in us while helping to make this manuscript a reality. We will never be able to thank you enough!

Contact

Team KO can be reached by email at SpartanTeamKo@gmail.com. We would love to hear from you!

MorganJames
Speakers Group

www.TheMorganJamesSpeakersGroup.com

We connect Morgan James published
authors with live and online events
and audiences who will benefit
from their expertise.

 Morgan James makes all of our titles available
through the Library for All Charity Organization.

www.LibraryForAll.org

CPSIA information can be obtained
at www.ICGtesting.com
Printed in the USA
LVOW12s2033170118
563092LV00002B/284/P